THE CAKE DECORATING BIBLE

Juliet Sear
of *Fancy Nancy*

THE CAKE DECORATING BIBLE

Juliet Sear
of *Fancy Nancy*

EBURY
PRESS

For Simon, George, Lydia and Ruby

10 9 8 7 6 5 4 3 2 1

Published in 2012 by Ebury Press, an imprint of Ebury Publishing

A Random House Group Company

Text copyright © Juliet Sear 2012
Photography copyright © Maja Smend 2012
(except pages 117, 157, 211 & 222 copyright © Dena Robles 2012
and page 140 copyright © Paul Tait 2012)

Juliet Sear has asserted her right to be identified as the author
of this Work in accordance with the Copyright, Designs and
Patents Act 1988

The Random House Group Limited Reg. No. 954009

Addresses for companies within the Random House Group
can be found at www.randomhouse.co.uk

A CIP catalogue record for this book is available from the
British Library

The Random House Group Limited supports The Forest
Stewardship Council® (FSC®), the leading international forest
certification organisation. Our books carrying the FSC label
are printed on FSC® certified paper. FSC is the only forest
certification scheme endorsed by the leading environmental
organisations, including Greenpeace. Our paper procurement
policy can be found at www.randomhouse.co.uk/environment

MIX
Paper from
responsible sources
FSC® C008047

Some of the recipes in this book contain ingredients such
as non toxic glitter which, whilst generally considered safe
for use, can be substituted with other or more traditional
ingredients. The author and publishers disclaim, as far as
the law allows, any liability arising directly or indirectly from
the use, or misuse, of the information contained in this book.

To buy books by your favourite authors and register for offers
visit www.randomhouse.co.uk

Colour origination: Altaimage, London
Printed and bound in China by C&C Offset Printing Co., Ltd

Design: Smith & Gilmour
Photography: Maja Smend,
(except pages 117, 157, 211 & 222, Dena Robles
and page 140, Paul Tait)
Prop styling: Alison Lovett

ISBN 9780091946685

CONTENTS

INTRODUCTION

I have always been interested in cooking and baking. When I met my husband I would cook up three-course meals with starters and puddings, partly, I think, to impress him, but mostly because I liked the feeling of achievement. Having a happy and adoring customer was also a good source of motivation.

My relationship with cakes, however, really started after I had my first child, over 13 years ago. Like many new mums, I was at home and had the urge to put on fairy-tale birthday parties, topped off with a great big, themed birthday cake: something that would impress the kids and probably the other mums as well. Teletubbies, Power Rangers, castles; whatever was in vogue at the time, I gave it a go.

I really enjoyed it and, before too long, admirers started to ask if I would bake and decorate cakes for them too. This turned into a little home business and within a few years I was baking weekly orders for a local café. It gave me some cash, a focus beyond my kids (I had three under the age of three) and a sense of enjoyment. However, I felt that the quality of my work was okay for an amateur but, having not had any formal training beyond home economics at school, I had reached a ceiling.

I got a bee in my bonnet about it, and over the next few years, whilst balancing commitments with the kids, I followed a short course at the Cordon Bleu cookery school, and undertook some work experience before getting a part-time job at the Little Venice Cake Company in Marylebone, London, where I worked for about 18 months.

In 2006 I set up my cake-making business, Fancy Nancy, trading from home for the first couple of years before moving into a shop with a bakery and decorating facilities in April 2009. These days, I have a team of half a dozen people and hundreds of customers. I get regular calls from magazines and TV producers for innovative designs and have made cakes for the likes of Eamonn Holmes, Dizzee Rascal, Holly Willoughby, Sir Ian McKellen, Richard Madeley, Bryan Adams, Fearne Cotton, Bob and Pixie Geldof....

It's been a long journey and not always easy. But despite the stress of it all, I really do enjoy designing and making cakes. I love the creativity of it and the fulfilment I get at seeing someone filled with joy when they come to pick up their cake or see it at their venue for the first time.

This book catalogues what I have learnt on the journey and passes on the methods that my team and I use in the Fancy Nancy kitchen every day. It explains techniques and shares trade secrets and clever shortcuts on how to get a perfect finish, how to bake the perfect chocolate cake, how to match the right cupcake sponge to topping, how to pick out the right design and a whole lot more.

Above and beyond everything, this book is full of practical know-how on creating shop-quality cakes in your own home.

CAKE JARGON AND SUPPLIES

In the world of cake decorating there are words, phrases and supplies that you may be unfamiliar with. Here they are explained.

ACETATE PAPER

A translucent, plastic, flexible paper that is used for creating run-outs. Because it is clear, you can trace images through it. If you find this hard to get hold of, you can use plastic stationery document wallets in its place.

BAKING PARCHMENT

A thick, moisture-proof, greaseproof paper used to line baking tins and trays. It can also be used to make piping bags.

BLEEDING

When one colour of icing runs or spreads into another; lighter-coloured icings can get stained by stronger ones. This happens most commonly with combinations of light and dark, especially on run-outs, or cookies decorated with royal icing.

BLOOMING

This is when chocolate gets unattractive white patches on its surface. The bloom can be caused by the fat or the sugar; the chocolate is still fine to eat and will still taste the same, but is less appealing to the eye. This can occasionally happen on a ganache cake if you keep it for a while.

BRUSH EMBROIDERY

A decorating technique where a piped royal-icing outline is brushed inwards with a soft, damp brush to create an embroidered effect.

CRUST OR SKIN OVER

A term used to describe when an icing surface or royal-icing run-outs start to dry out and form a hard crust on the surface. This prevents one colour from staining another; in cake decorating you often have to wait for this to happen before moving on to the next step.

DUST COLOURS

These are non-toxic powders, available in many colours and shades. You can use them to decorate dried sugar decorations or they can be mixed with vodka or cocoa butter to create a paint that you can use for cake decorating. You can apply them with a dry brush to give your sugar decorations more depth and varied colours.

EDIBLE-INK CARTRIDGES

Cartridges filled with edible ink (food colouring), which can be used with a normal printer as long as the printer is used for edible ink only.

EDIBLE PAPER/EDIBLE SHEETS

Edible paper made from sugar. As well as being used in edible-ink printers to produce edible pictures and patterns, it can be airbrushed, and easily cut into shapes, e.g. for fairy wings.

FLOODING

This is when you fill in a royal-icing outline with a more liquid royal-icing colour, to give blocks or shapes of colour to decorate a cookie or cake. This is how run-outs are made.

FORMERS

These are solid forms or shapes used to dry sugar flowers, leaves or pieces, e.g. sugar shoes on. You can buy plastic formers for many purposes or indeed make your own using old, dry sugarpaste wrapped in cling film, or even using folded card.

GANACHE

A mixture of chocolate and cream used for filling or covering a cake.

GLITTERISING

When you apply non-toxic glitter to the surface of a cake, cookie or sugar decoration to add magical sparkliness. Non-toxic glitter is considered safe to use, but if you prefer not to use glitter, you can substitute it with 'sanding sugars'. These are coloured sugars that glimmer but are not as sparkly as glitter (see page 9).

GLYCERINE

Glycerine is a sweet, clear, odourless syrup that is available in supermarkets and from cake-decorating suppliers. It is a softening agent that is extracted from fats and oils, and in cake decorating it is primarily used as an addition to royal icing, to prevent the icing from becoming too hard, allowing you to cut through the iced covering more easily. Without it, royal icing sets rock-hard and will break up when a knife is inserted into the cake.

GUIDE STICKS OR MARZIPAN SPACERS

You can buy these from sugarcraft suppliers; they are used to ensure an even thickness when rolling out sugarpaste, marzipan, chocolate coatings or cookie dough.

GUM ARABIC

When gum arabic is mixed with water, it can be used as a glaze for marzipan, or as edible glue for sugarpaste. As a glaze, it gives the decoration a glossy sheen.

GUM TRAGACANTH

This is a plant-derived chemical that can be used to stiffen sugarpaste to make it set harder and hold its shape. It's particularly handy for modelling, when you need shapes to stay in form.

LEVELLING

To make your cake or icing level on the surface.

LIQUID GLUCOSE

Also known as glucose syrup, this is a viscous sugar solution of glucose suspended in liquid, which is sold in jars or tubs. It is now more readily available and can be bought from the baking section of supermarkets, from chemists, or from chocolate and baking suppliers. It is used to make chocolate paste, as when added to chocolate, it allows the chocolate to be moulded or rolled out.

LUSTRE DUST

Lustre dusts are non-toxic powders that come in many different colours and metallic shades. Sugar flowers, embellishments or iced surfaces can be decorated with lustre to give them a twinkling, metallic effect.

Lustre dusts can be mixed with vodka or cocoa butter and painted directly onto sugar decorations or a cake itself, though the dust can also be applied dry.

LUSTRE SPRAY

An edible spray that can be used to decorate and add sheen to a cake's surface or to sugar decorations to give a metallic sheen. It is much quicker than painting on lustre dust.

MARBLING

When two or more colours of icing are added to a base coat of Royal icing, and a cocktail stick is then dragged through them to create a swirly, patterned effect.

PALETTE KNIFE

A tool used to spread and smooth fillings or icings.

PASTE COLOURING

Professional, strong, cake-decorating colourings with a paste or gel-like consistency that is stronger and more intense than liquid food colouring, and does not affect the consistency of sugarpaste or liquid icings. You can buy these from cake-decorating suppliers or online, and even some supermarkets are now starting to stock them.

PEARLS

Small round piped dots of royal icing.

PETAL PASTE

A stiff sugarpaste that is used for making flowers. It can be rolled very thinly and sets rock-hard, so that petals look less chunky and more realistic. It dries out very quickly. I also use this for making sugar buttons.

PIPING

When you force royal icing, buttercream or melted chocolate out of a bag through a nozzle, to create a message, add detail or texturise a cake.

PIPING BAG OR PASTRY BAG

Cone-shaped bags made out of plastic, fabric or paper, used for piping royal icing, buttercream and melted chocolate. You can buy these easily or save money by making your own using baking parchment (see page 26). They can be used by themselves or with piping nozzles.

PIPING GEL

A sugary gel that can be used for many different aspects of cake decorating, including glazing sugarpaste or to give a sheen. It can be tinted with colours or added to metallic lustres to give cakes a shiny finish. You can also use it to create novelty effects, such as the suggestion of water. I prefer the Squires Kitchen brand because the gel is clearer and much easier to apply than many.

PIPING NOZZLES, TUBES OR TIPS

Used for piping lines, swirls, flowers, patterns and messages onto cakes using royal icing, buttercream or melted chocolate. I recommend only stainless-steel nozzles, as these are much better quality than the plastic variety. Piping nozzles come in many shapes and sizes, including circle, star or leaf-tip openings, allowing the user to pipe different shapes and create various effects. The simple round-tip nozzles come in standard sizes that indicate the dimension of the opening; all cake-decorating suppliers and online stores use the same sizes. For example, piping nozzles used for writing and lace embroidery are either No. 2 or No. 3, which have 2mm and 3mm openings respectively. No. 1 or No. 1.5 nozzles can be used for very fine detail, such as tiny pearls in a lace pattern, linear patterns or facial details on small figurines. The star or flower-shaped nozzles come in a variety of different shapes and most catalogues and websites offer a visual guide or drawing as to what kind of iced effect each tip will produce.

PLUNGER CUTTER

A cake-decorating cutter that cuts out, then ejects, a shape. These are now available in many different shapes; they are quick and easy to use.

PRESSURE PIPING

A piping technique that uses varying amounts of pressure to create a more shaped piped line, with thicker parts in the pattern that trail off to thinner parts, and vice versa.

ROLLED FONDANT

Another name for sugarpaste (see below).

ROYAL ICING

A white or coloured liquid icing that sets hard. It is made with icing sugar, egg white and lemon juice, and can have glycerine added to it when being used to cover a cake, to keep it softer and slightly easier to cut through. It is a fairly old-fashioned cake covering (rolled pastes are more commonly used nowadays).

RUN-OUT

This is a decoration or shape made by piping a border or outline with royal icing, then filling or 'flooding' the outlined areas with a more liquid royal icing, in whatever colours you like. Also known as flood work, these can be piped onto baking parchment or acetate paper or directly onto the surface of a cookie or cake. When the shape is dry, you have an icing decoration that can be used in many ways. You can even make run-outs on wires, cocktail sticks or skewers so that they can stand upright on a cake.

SANDING SUGAR

A large, granular sugar that comes in many colours and is used for cookie decorating or cake decorating to create a sparkly look.

SCORING

Scribing onto a cake to give you a guideline for writing over, marking out a shape or making a mark to indicate where you want to place a decoration or cake tier.

SILICONE OR PUSH MOULDS

Flexible moulds for making quick sugarpaste models, e.g. flowers, to use as decorations for the top of cakes and cupcakes. They come in hundreds of designs, including silicone moulds for giving sugarpaste a lace or textured pattern.

SNAGGING

When you get a rough finish or peak on icing pearls or trails, or a dent in the icing surface. You can correct snags by patting down rough peaks with a small, damp, clean paintbrush or by filling holes and dents with royal icing.

SNAIL TRAIL

When icing is piped around a cake in a continuous line, using any kind of nozzle to create a textured or shaped trailing line to finish or decorate.

SOFT PEAK

A term used to describe the consistency of royal icing. When the icing is lifted from the bowl with the back of a spoon or palette knife, it will have a peak that droops down and won't hold a stiff shape.

SPLITTING AND FILLING

Cutting a cake horizontally and sandwiching the two halves together with a flavoured filling, usually buttercream.

STIFF PEAK

A term used to describe royal icing mixed to a consistency that is stiff enough to hold a firm peak when lifted from the bowl with the back of a spoon or palette knife.

SUGARPASTE (OR ROLLED FONDANT)

An icing paste made from icing sugar, water and gelatin. It is usually purchased rather than made from scratch, as you can buy great-quality ready-made fondant. It is used for covering cakes and boards, and for making flowers, shapes and models.

TAIL

A tiny tail-like projection that forms on the tip of a piped pearl when the nozzle is lifted away. This spoils the roundness of your pearl; it can be rectified by patting down gently with a small, damp, clean paintbrush.

TEXTURISING

A method of adding a rough pattern or detailed finish to a cake.

VEINER

A rubber, plastic or silicone mould that can be used for marking and making impressions onto petal paste or sugarpaste to make leaves or flowers look more realistic. Some plunger cutters will cut out a shape and also make an impression at the same time, which saves the need for a separate veiner.

EQUIPMENT AND TOOLS

There are many fantastic things you can do with a minimum amount of cake decorating 'stuff'. I have learnt over the years that if you haven't got certain pieces of equipment, there are often handy things that you can substitute. When we've got a few cakes on the go at Fancy Nancy and run out of equipment, we often find ingenious solutions. And if you are just starting out you might not want to go and spend loads of money on tools, so it helps if you can adapt things you already have. For example, an upturned cake tin, book or bowl will work as a makeshift turntable. Therefore, throughout this book, I have suggested ways to improvise without the specified kit whenever possible.

However, as with anything, if you want to increase your repertoire then you need to invest time, and if you want to get quicker – and make the job easier – you need to get yourself a few pieces of invaluable kit. If you took up photography, you'd need a camera; for windsurfing you'd need a board and sail. The surge of interest in home baking and cake decorating has fuelled a huge increase in the amount of equipment available for cake decorators. There are some really innovative bits of kit on offer and it is worth investing in some of these useful tools if you have reached the stage of wanting to expand your cake-decorating horizons.

There is also a wide variety of exciting edible supplies you can use to make your cakes look amazing. It's incredible what you can get, from gorgeous glitters in every imaginable colour to sugar decorations in hundreds of shapes, sizes and colours and edible prints or metallic embellishments. The list is endless and ever-expanding as the cake-decorating market grows. Of course, once you get into cake decorating you may want to make your own versions of these but there is a huge array of ready-made sugar designs out there for the beginner to use in their own way on a lovingly-baked creation.

In this section I have listed the tools I refer to in this book as well as a few extra bits and pieces. I have also explained how to improvise without them whenever it is possible to do this.

BASICS AND BAKING

- A good-quality electric mixer (e.g. Kitchen Aid, Kenwood). You can use a hand mixer if you are short on cash, but it is really worth investing if you are serious about cake-making and decorating

- Mixing bowls in a range of sizes

- Wooden spoons

- Metal tablespoons and teaspoons

- Knives: large bread knife for cutting, splitting and filling cakes; large serrated knife; small sharp knife

Large, medium and small palette knives – perfect for covering, spreading and carefully lifting up cakes

Spatula

Sieve

Whisk

Cake leveller

Scissors

Pastry brushes

Cake tins in various shapes and sizes

Muffin/cupcake trays

Paper muffin cases

Cookie cutters – can also be used for cutting sugarpaste

Lolly/cookie sticks – for making lollipops or the Cookie Explosion cake on page 217

Non-stick baking parchment or paper (avoid normal greaseproof)

Weighing scales – I recommend digital scales for the most accurate measurements, as it's important to be precise with baking recipes

CAKE DECORATING

Must-haves:

Rolling pins (ideally plastic) – a large one for rolling out coverings for the top and sides of a cake (should be 8cm/3in larger than the diameter of the cake, so for a 20cm/8in cake a 35cm/14in) rolling pin is best) and a small plastic pin (15–20cm/ 6–8in), for rolling out small amounts of sugarpaste, or especially petal paste, for decorating

Cake boards

Piping bags

Piping nozzles/tubes – these come in many sizes but a basic set includes No. 2 and No. 3 round nozzles and a simple star nozzle. It's easy to make your own leaf-tip nozzle by cutting down a piping bag to create a 'V' shape at the end.

Scriber needle or pin tool (or use a regular pin with a ball head, but take care not to lose it!) – this is used for popping air bubbles, removing tiny particles or colour marks and marking out lettering or patterns on your cake

Nice-to-haves:

Turntable

Guide sticks or marzipan spacers – not essential but handy for ensuring an even thickness to cake coverings and cookie dough

Side scraper (or a small plastic ruler as an alternative)

- Straight edge tool (you can use a metal or strong plastic ruler instead, but those generally only go up to 30cm/12in, so you can't use them for cakes that are any bigger)

- Cake smoothers: ideally two side smoothers and one top smoother

- Varying sizes of paintbrushes for dusting colours, painting and fixing mistakes

- Ribbon cutter – a handy, wheeled cutter that can be adjusted to cut different width strips of sugarpaste, chocolate or petal paste, as well as ribbon

- Ribbons

- Cake dowels – for stacking cakes. I find the extra-strong heavy-duty ones are the best option, especially for your base cake if you are stacking a few tiers

- Polystyrene cake dummies – shaped polystyrene 'fake' cakes. They come in many shapes besides round and square and are usually 7.5cm (3in) in depth

- Polystyrene separators – polystyrene squares or circles of a shallower depth than cake dummies; they come in 2.5cm (1in) and 5cm (2in) depths

- Projector – some people like to project images onto a cake's surface to aid with hand-painting or piping. It is not essential but great if you aren't good at freehand drawing and painting. Alternatively, you can print off a picture and mark out the edges by stabbing carefully through the paper with a pin to create a dotted line on the icing, then all you have to do is 'join the dots' with icing!

SUGARCRAFT MODELLING TOOLS

- Sugarcraft cutters – rose, blossom, daisy, calyx and leaf cutters, including plain metal cutters and also plunger-style cutters

- Silicone moulds and push moulds

- Foam or gel pad – this provides a soft surface to press against when making impressions on petal-paste shapes such as buttons or leaves, when frilling petals, or using plunger cutters; it ensures you get the veining or pattern from the plunger cutter

- Floppy mat – for covering petal paste to prevent it from drying out (you can use a large book wrapped in cling film as an alternative)

- Ball or bone tool – I find this invaluable and you'll need it for making buttons

- Dresden tool – a narrow, stick-like, plastic or wooden tool with tapered, spike-like ends, used in modelling to create lines, indentations and impressions, for example on a petal

- Scalpel

- Quilting or stitching wheels – handy little tools with removable wheels that give different effects

PACKAGING AND TRANSPORTATION

- Cake boxes

- Cupcake boxes

- Individual cupcake or portion boxes

- Cookie bags (I recently saw these in a supermarket baking section, or you can order from a specialist supplier)

PREPARATION: CAKE AND COOKIE BASICS

In order to produce perfect cakes or cookies at home, there are simple steps that you should follow to make sure that you get the best result. It's worth spending a few minutes on these steps; don't rush, as they can make life much easier in the long run.

With baking, and particularly cake decorating, you do need to invest your time. It's different from other types of cooking; you aren't just throwing together a quick spag bol or curry. It will take a bit more time and care, and sometimes needs to be spread out over a couple of days or more, but it's worth the effort because it's so rewarding.

CHOOSING A CAKE TIN

If you can, invest in a good tin to bake your cake in. At Fancy Nancy we use Invicta tins – the beauty of these is that they are all exactly the same height, 8cm (3in), which is a perfect depth for a celebration or wedding cake. We use this height as a guide for all our sponge cakes.

Of course you can use any tins, but if you are making a stacked cake, you want all the sponge tiers to be the same height so that the cake doesn't look odd. So do try to buy cake tins of the same depth if you want to try out my easy, foolproof method for preparing the sponges. You can still get good results with other tins, but when it comes to cake decorating, time saving and foolproofing are very important to me.

LINING CAKE TINS AND COOKIE TRAYS

Always line your tins and trays, as it will prevent the cakes and cookies from becoming stuck. If you don't, you may have to use a knife to free the cake from its tin and end up with chunks of your cake getting hacked off, resulting in a bumpy surface under your icing – not a good look. You will be pretty hacked off yourself about having to patch up all the holes before you start decorating. So it's worth spending the time to do this right to ensure you get the best result.

Make sure you use silicon baking parchment for lining, not greaseproof paper. Greaseproof paper isn't substantial enough and often disintegrates, or gets baked onto the tin and sticks to the cake. Parchment will protect your sponge, save on washing-up and easily peel away from your sponge. You can find parchment in the baking section of supermarkets or alongside the cling film and foil.

LINING ROUND TINS

STEP 1 First, generously grease your cake tin with plenty of butter by smudging it all over with a piece of kitchen paper, a pastry brush or even with your fingers.

STEP 2 To line the sides, cut long strips of baking parchment approximately 10cm (4in) in depth (with the length of the strips determined by the width of the roll); this will mean that the parchment rises a couple of centimetres higher than the sides of the tin. Cut as many strips as you need: for example, a 15cm (6in) tin will probably need just one strip, but a 30cm (12in) tin will take two or three strips.

STEP 3 Put all your strips on top of each other and fold over 1cm (½in) along one long edge. With scissors, make lots of snips all along this folded part, at 90 degrees to the fold line and snipping just up to the crease, to create a 'fringed' edge.

STEP 4 Separate the strips and place onto the internal wall of the tin, with the snipped part sitting flat on the base.

STEP 5 Sit the tin on top of the rolled-out baking parchment and either cut with a sharp knife all the way round (if your worktop or surface is safe to cut onto) or draw a circle around the tin and cut out with scissors. Place the parchment disc into the base of the tin, overlaying the snipped, folded edge that's sitting around the sides. Now your tin is perfectly lined and ready for your cake batter.

TIP

You can bake the cakes the day before you need them and leave at room temperature, or you can make them a few days in advance, then wrap well and chill or even freeze them if necessary. Just make sure that you defrost them thoroughly one day before use.

LINING SQUARE OR OBLONG TINS

STEP 1 First, generously grease your cake tin with plenty of butter by smudging it all over with a piece of kitchen paper, a pastry brush or even with your fingers.

STEP 2 Line three of the sides by cutting strips of baking parchment to the correct length and approximately 10cm (4in) in depth; the strips will rise a couple of centimetres higher than the sides of the tin.

STEP 3 Fold over 1cm (½in) along one long edge of each strip. With scissors, make lots of snips all along this folded part, at 90 degrees to the fold line, just up to the crease, to create a 'fringed' edge. Place the strips onto three of the internal walls of the tin, with the snipped edges sitting flat on the base.

STEP 4 Sit the tin on top of the rolled-out baking parchment, lined up to one edge.

STEP 5 Cut round the tin, but allow about 10cm (4in) extra for the side that hasn't yet been lined. When you place this piece of paper into the base of the tin, the extra-long edge can be folded up to line the final side. Now you have a perfectly lined tin ready to bake your sponge.

LINING COOKIE TRAYS

When you are baking cookies for decorating, I really recommend that you line the trays with baking parchment so that the cookies don't stick. It will damage their shape if you have to try to unstick them from the tray with a knife. When using baking parchment, they will easily glide off.

Simply cut a piece of baking parchment to fit the tray you are using. To stop it sliding around on the tray, stick it down by dampening the tray with a bit of water so that the paper clings to it. Alternatively, you can dab a bit of royal icing in each corner to fix the parchment in place.

FILLING YOUR TINS

Once your tins are lined, you are ready to start baking your sponges – whatever flavours you decide upon – ready for decorating. That's the crucial thing to bear in mind here: you aren't baking a simple sponge to layer and eat in its naked (but gorgeous) state. You want to decorate this cake. So you need to start with a good base.

When baking a cake for decorating, unless it's for a design that will be covered entirely in some form of sugar, chocolate or cookie embellishment, you should aim for a smooth and uniform shape, a flat surface and, importantly, straight edges and a level top. Of course, if your sponge isn't perfect, you can always patch it up, and add layers of marzipan or sugarpaste to get the cake base nice and even, but that can take a good 30–60 minutes for an average-sized sponge, so it's best avoided.

Getting the top of the cake flat is one of the first things you need to make happen. This top tip came from my good old dad, George (an engineer by trade who is ever present in the kitchen, adapting his inventive ideas into cake-decorating tips), and it makes this laborious stage so much easier.

As described in the tin-lining instructions, line your tin so that there's an extra inch of baking parchment poking up above the top edge. Then fill the tin with cake batter almost right to the top, just about 1cm (½in) below the edge. This will allow your sponge to rise above the top of the tin. Once cooled, you can put the cake back into its tin and slice off the top using the tin as a guide. This gives a perfect flat result, ready to decorate without the hassle of reshaping, patching or building up. (Note that this tip only applies to the Very Vanilla and Lemon Drizzle recipes; the Rich Belgian Chocolate Truffle cake cannot be baked like this.)

Not only does this save time later (and you can be doing other things whilst the sponge is in the oven), but it will also give you a perfect base on which to decorate.

For all of the cupcakes in this book, I have used a muffin-sized cupcake tray in which the muffin cup measures 51 x 38mm (51mm diameter and 38mm deep). If you are using a different size, you will need to adjust the amount of cake mixture – as a guide, I fill the cases half full for buttercream-topped cupcakes, and one-third full for cupcakes that will be covered with fondant or ganache, so that it will sit fairly flat, rather than having a domed top.

My sponge recipes take a bit longer than regular ones because they are quite deep, so they need longer to cook in the centre. All ovens vary, so once you have filled the tin right up with batter, bake it at the usual temperature (around 200°C/Gas mark 6 depending on your oven) for the first 30 minutes, until the cake has risen nice and high, up to the top of the baking parchment. Once it's well risen, turn the oven down by about 10°C/one gas mark.

With a small sponge of this depth, up to a diameter of 18cm (7in), you will need to cook it for approximately 20 minutes extra than with usual sponge recipes, but larger 25cm (10in) sponges take up to 45–60 minutes extra. You therefore need to make sure that the edges don't burn before the middle cooks through. For these larger sponges, once I have cooked them for an extra 30 minutes or so at about 190°C/Gas mark 3, I then turn the oven down to around 170°C/ Gas mark 2. By this point, the sponge will have risen and set, but this extra-low cooking temperature allows the centre to cook through until dry when tested with a skewer or sharp knife. (If you are using shallower tins than mine, use your judgement and keep a close eye on your sponge throughout the baking, checking it regularly.)

The chocolate sponge is not baked in this way as it is really dense and fudgy and if you baked it for too long you would lose the wonderful velvety chocolateyness of the cake. Instead, you need to bake it in two halves.

PRE-ICING YOUR CAKE BOARDS

Many of the designs in this book are displayed on an iced board. This gives your cakes a professional touch and makes sure the design looks complete. I think it looks really messy if you place a beautiful cake onto an un-iced cake board with the silver foil showing.

Icing cake boards with sugarpaste is easy and, because sugarpaste has a very long shelf life, it can be done way in advance, saving time when you are making and decorating the actual cake. It is best done at least 24 hours before you want to put your cake onto the board, so that the sugarpaste is dry and doesn't get squeezed over the edge by the weight of the cake.

Cakes are usually placed on a board that is 5–8cm (2–3in) larger than the cake itself, unless your design involves lots of decoration or models, etc. on the board, in which case you may want a larger one. You might wish to cover it with the same colour icing that you will use to decorate your cake, or perhaps choose a contrasting colour.

To cover a 30cm (12in) round cake board you will need approximately 750g sugarpaste. Below is a handy table to give you a guide to the amounts of sugarpaste you will need for icing different-sized cake boards.

CAKE BOARD	15cm (6in) round	15cm (6in) square	20cm (8in) round	20cm (8in) square	25cm (10in) round	25cm (10in) square
Sugarpaste	300g	375g	550g	650g	650g	750g
CAKE BOARD	30cm (12in) round	30cm (12in) square	35cm (14in) round	35cm (14in) square	40cm (16in) round	40cm (16in) square
Sugarpaste	750g	900g	1kg	1.25kg	1.25kg	1.5kg

STEP 1 These instructions are for a round cake board; the same principles apply for a square board. Dust the cake board with a little icing sugar, then wet this with a pastry brush dipped in cooled boiled water or vodka – this will stick the icing to the board so that it doesn't slide around while you are trimming off the edges.

STEP 2 Knead the sugarpaste until pliable, then shape into a ball and flatten. Before rolling out, dust the worktop beneath the icing with plenty of icing sugar. You can also dust the top of the sugarpaste with

just a little icing sugar but try not to use too much or the sugarpaste will become dry and can easily crack.

STEP 3 Roll out the sugarpaste evenly from the middle outwards, turning it regularly to prevent an uneven or spidery shape; you want a nice round piece to lay over the cake board. You can use guide sticks if you have them, otherwise take care to roll with even pressure so that the sugarpaste has a good, even thickness of approximately 5–6mm.

STEP 4 Once rolled, lift the sugarpaste carefully over both arms, or roll it onto your pin to lift, and place on your dampened cake board. (If you haven't quite judged the size right and you have too little icing or the shape isn't quite round, you can easily strip it off the board and re-roll it.) Make sure that there are no air bubbles under the icing – you should be able to see them if you bend down so that the board is at eye level. If you see any, use a pin tool or scriber tool to pierce a small hole in the icing and gently expel the air by pushing it out with your fingertips.

If you get too much icing sugar on the surface of a dark-coloured sugarpaste, especially black, the icing sugar will cause white blotches that spoil the iced surface and are very hard to remove — if this happens, re-knead and roll the sugarpaste again.

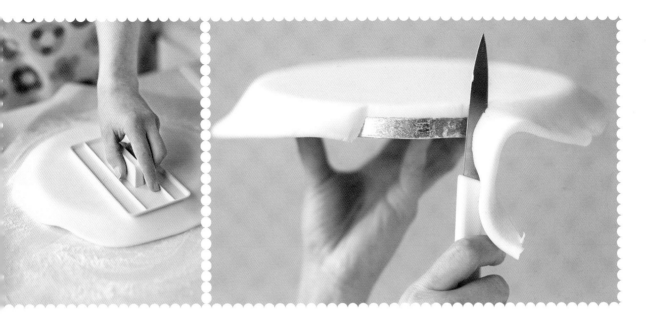

STEP 5 Now smooth over the board with a top smoother (or with the flat of your hand, but a smoother guarantees a better finish), to iron out any lumps and bumps and to polish and smooth the sugarpaste.

STEP 6 Finally, you need to trim off the excess. Hold up the cake board with one hand (as you would hold a plate, with your fingers splayed out under the board). With a sharp knife, carefully cut all the way around the edge, holding the knife at a 90-degree angle to the board and using the edge as a guide. Let the excess sugarpaste fall back onto the worktop; you can re-use this. Turn the cake board as you cut, until you have gone all the way around the board.

STEP 7 When you have trimmed off the excess icing, make sure the edge is neat and that there are no rough bits, by gently smoothing round the board with your fingertips. Leave the board aside to dry until needed, for at least 24 hours.

TIP

If you find it tricky holding the board in one hand, another option is to use a turntable. Place the board on the turntable, make an initial cut into the excess sugarpaste, then hold the knife in place. Now rotate the board so that your knife glides through the rest.

MAKING PIPING BAGS

For cake decorating you will need lots of piping bags. Of course, you can easily buy disposable ones, but it's handy (and cheaper) if you can make your own. If you want to ice a cake with a variety of different colours, it's best to make plenty of piping bags before you start, as you'll need a separate bag for each colour. I keep a stock of them, and make 100 or so at once, so that I have them ready for whenever I need them.

Ideally use baking parchment for making these, as it is stronger and more substantial than greaseproof paper and so will last longer. For instance, if you load a bag with coloured royal icing and have some left over, you might want to use the rest the next day. With greaseproof, you may find that the bag splits. Parchment, on the other hand, is coated, so it won't get too soggy from the icing. (However, if greaseproof is all you have, then just use it.)

STEP 1 Unroll the parchment and cut at intervals, so that you end up with several large squares of parchment.

STEP 2 Cut across each square on the diagonal from corner to corner. You will be left with large triangles of paper.

STEP 3 Place a triangle with the longest straight edge away from you and the opposite point facing towards you, then take hold of one outer corner (I start on the right-hand side, but this depends on whether you are left- or right-handed), and bring it in to meet the point. Pull this in tightly so that a cone shape begins to form.

STEP 4 Hold these corners together tightly and lift up the cone in front of you. Bring the other corner in by wrapping it around behind the cone, to meet your thumb that's holding the first part together. Quickly and carefully slip the new corner under your thumb too, making sure not to let go of the other bit.

STEP 5 Check you have a sharp point at the end of your bag: if it's not sharp you can play with it by pulling the cone tighter with your thumbs and fingers. If you don't get it right the first time, keep trying; it's easy once you get the hang of it but it does take a few goes to get the feel of it.

STEP 6 To secure the piping bag, staple it at the top of the cone where the paper is overlapping. This is the best method, but do take care that no stray staples fall into your piping bag or find their way into your cake.

RECIPES

CHAPTER 1

The following sponge recipes produce cakes that are perfect for decorating. They are delicious yet robust and firm enough to be cut, carved, split and filled and will hold the weight of your marzipan and sugarpaste or chocolate paste. I bake these recipes all the time, but of course if you are making these for the first time, do take extra care and be sure to check your cake regularly whilst its is cooking, as all ovens vary and you will need to find what works for your oven.

With all my recipes, I truly believe that if you buy the best-quality ingredients that you can, you will achieve a better finished product. I like to use free-range organic eggs and organic flour, sugar and butter, but of course you can't always get hold of these or justify the cost. At the very least, buy free-range eggs if you can afford to.

VERY VANILLA SPONGE

This gorgeous springy vanilla sponge is so incredibly versatile. You can use it as the basis for all kinds of cakes — from a large Victoria sponge to cupcakes (see variation), and it's special enough for celebration or wedding cakes. See the quantities chart overleaf for a guide to making larger mixes to fill different sizes of tins, should you want to make a selection of tiers for one of the larger stacked cakes in the book. You can also make double, triple or even a litre of the syrup if you bake often or are tackling one of the tiered cake designs.

Whenever I have customers in for wedding-cake consultations and they try this cake, their eyes widen and they ask how it's so much lovelier than a 'normal' sponge. It is loaded with vanilla — I like to use vanilla seeds plus vanilla extract, a good-quality one to give it a real headiness. Then, to add an extra vanilla kick, I drizzle the top of the warm sponge with vanilla sugar syrup, which is easy to make and store; not only does this add to the sweet flavour but it also keeps the cake moist and prolongs its shelf life. Once you and your friends have tasted the results — and discovered how easy it is to make — you will want to make it over and over again.

Having all your ingredients at room temperature makes your cake batter come together perfectly. If your ingredients are cold, they will not combine well and the eggs may curdle.

MAKES A 15CM (6IN) ROUND CAKE

For the vanilla syrup
100g golden caster sugar
100ml water
1 vanilla pod, seeds scraped into a bowl
  and pod saved

For the vanilla sponge
200g softened butter
200g golden caster sugar
1 vanilla pod, seeds scraped into a bowl
1 tsp good-quality vanilla extract
  (I love Neilson Massey)
4 medium eggs, lightly beaten
200g self-raising flour

STEP 1 Preheat the oven to 180°C/Gas mark 4. Line a 15cm (6in) round cake tin with baking parchment (see page 19).

STEP 2 To make the syrup, mix the sugar and water in a saucepan and bring gently to the boil, stirring occasionally to prevent lumps or burning. Once it starts to boil, remove from the heat and allow to cool slightly. Alternatively, you can microwave the sugar and water for 1 minute at a time until all the sugar crystals have dissolved and the syrup has boiled.) Add the seeds from the scraped vanilla pod and then add the pod for extra vanilla flavour. Leave to infuse. Once cool, transfer to a squeezy bottle or jug for pouring.

STEP 3 To make the sponge, combine the butter, sugar, vanilla seeds and extract and beat with a wooden spoon, hand mixer or in an electric mixer on medium–fast speed, until the mixture is very pale, soft and fluffy and the granules of sugar have disappeared.

STEP 4 Add the beaten eggs, a quarter at a time. If it curdles a little (looks lumpy and separated) just add a spoonful of flour from your weighed-out amount. Mix this in slowly with each addition.

STEP 5 Then add the flour gradually, a quarter at a time, gently stirring it in as you go. Slowly mix until the dry flour has been mostly mixed in. Don't mix it too quickly or over-process the flour, or the sponge can turn out a bit chewy.

STEP 6 Spoon the cake mixture into the lined cake tin, pushing it up the edges a bit, so that the sponge will rise high in the tin. Create a well in the centre to prevent a large hump from rising; this will help your sponge to rise evenly.

STEP 7 Bake for 35–40 minutes (but check on it after 30 minutes, as all ovens vary). You want a nice, high sponge, and test with a knife to be sure the middle is cooked through. You might need to cook it for longer; even for up to an hour. If you think the outside is cooking too fast, turn the oven down and cover the top with a piece of foil to prevent it burning. Once the sponge is very risen and beginning to firm up, you can turn your oven down to 160°C.

STEP 8 When cooked, turn out onto a wire rack and peel off the paper to allow steam to evaporate from the sponge. Whilst still warm, spear through the crust in several places with a sharp knife or skewer, then drizzle or brush the sponge with the syrup. To feed the syrup into the holes you can use a pastry brush or a squeezy sauce bottle or drizzle it slowly from a jug with a spout. You don't want it too soggy but you need enough to soak in: use around 60ml for the top of the cake, and save the rest to use in the middle of the cake when you later split it to be filled. Now leave the cake to cool completely.

See pages 61–63 for instructions on splitting and filling the cake.

SHELF LIFE AND STORAGE

Either use straight away or store by wrapping in plenty of cling film and chilling for up to 3 days. Or you can freeze for up to 3 months. Once iced, the vanilla sponge will keep fresh for up to 5 days; it will of course remain safe to eat for a while afterwards but you will find that it becomes dry and less palatable over time. As with most food products, it is best eaten as soon as possible.

The vanilla syrup will keep in the fridge for up to 2 weeks. You can also freeze it; pour portions of around 100ml into small freezer bags to use as and when you need them (take out the night before to defrost).

If making one of the bigger cake sizes, you may need to divide large quantities into two bowls or batches, or else your mixture might overflow.

VERY VANILLA SPONGE QUANTITIES CHART

	15cm (6in) round	20cm (8in) round / 15cm (6in) square	25cm (10in) round / 20cm (8in) square	30cm (12in) round / 25cm (10in) square	30cm (12in) square
Softened butter	200g	400g	700g	800g	1kg
Golden caster sugar	200g	400g	700g	800g	1kg
Vanilla pod	1	1½	2.5	3	3.5-4
Vanilla extract	1 tsp	2 tsp	3 tsp (1 tbsp)	4 tsp	5 tsp
Medium eggs, beaten	4	8	14	16	20
Self-raising flour	200g	400g	700g	800g	1kg
180°C/ Gas mark 4	35–40 mins	50 mins– 1 hr	1 hr 15 mins– 1 hr 30 mins	1 hr 30 mins– 2 hrs	2 hrs – 2 hrs 30 mins

One batch of the syrup will still be enough for all the above sizes of cake. Use the syrup to taste, brushing it over each layer of cake without soaking them. How much you need is really down to personal taste. Be careful, though, the cake can become sugary if too much syrup is used.

Begin checking the bake after 30 minutes and check periodically, as ovens vary greatly and the gauge of tin can also affect this. Always check if the sponge is baked through by inserting a skewer or sharp knife into the centre.

VERY VANILLA CUPCAKES

MAKES 12–16 CUPCAKES

STEP 1 Preheat the oven to 200°C/Gas mark 6. Line one or two 12-hole muffin trays with paper muffin cases.

STEP 2 Follow steps 1–5 of the main vanilla sponge recipe, then divide the mixture between the cases and cook for 10–15 minutes. Check after 10 minutes, as all ovens vary; the cakes should be a light golden brown and springy to touch. If you want to be sure, test with a sharp knife – this should come out clean and free of mixture if they are cooked through.

STEP 3 Once baked, turn the cakes out onto a cooling rack and brush or drizzle with a little vanilla syrup to coat the tops and soak into your sponges. (You will have more syrup than you need, as the amount in the main recipe covers about 30 cupcakes, but you can't really make it in smaller quantities. See page 32 for storing any leftovers.) Leave the cakes to cool, then decorate as required.

SHELF LIFE AND STORAGE

These can be frozen, but take care not to knock the paper cases, or they will look messy if you later want to add fondant or ganache. Freeze in a container to help protect them. Alternatively, you can leave the cooled cakes in their baking tin, wrap the whole tin in cling film and freeze. This also ensures they won't get squashed. Once iced, the cakes will last well for 3–4 days.

RICH BELGIAN CHOCOLATE TRUFFLE CAKE

This cake is to die for ... I've tried lots of good chocolate cake recipes and have tweaked my favourites until I got this result. It's soft, fudgy and decadent, but there's enough flour in the mixture for it to keep its shape when being cut, without crumbling too much — the perfect balance of taste and practicality. You will have some leftover sponge from baking this cake, as you need to cut off the top crust from both halves. Save these gorgeous bits to put in trifles or eat with ice cream. See the quantities chart overleaf for a guide to baking other sizes, if you want to make multiple tiers.

MAKES A 15CM (6IN) ROUND CAKE
240g plain chocolate chips, 70% cocoa solids
300g softened unsalted butter
420g soft light brown sugar
6 medium eggs, beaten
1 tsp good-quality vanilla extract
240g plain flour

STEP 1 Preheat the oven to 160°C/Gas mark 3. Line two 15cm (6in) round tins (you can't make this sponge in one tin as it's too heavy; you need to cook it in two halves) with baking parchment (see page 19).

STEP 2 Melt the chocolate in the microwave on medium heat for a minute at a time, stirring at each interval. Alternatively, melt it in a heatproof bowl set over a pan of just-simmering water. Leave to cool.

STEP 3 Beat the butter and sugar together slowly with an electric hand mixer or in an electric mixer (or in a large bowl with a wooden spoon) until combined, then beat vigorously on a fast speed until the mixture turns pale, soft and fluffy.

STEP 4 Add the beaten eggs a little at a time, mixing slowly until each addition is incorporated.

STEP 5 Pour the cooled chocolate into your mixture, beating all the time until everything is combined.

STEP 6 Stir or mix in the vanilla extract with the mixer on slow.

STEP 7 Add the flour and fold or mix in slowly, until it's combined with the wet ingredients.

STEP 8 Spoon evenly into the lined tins. You need to fill each tin around 6cm (2½in) deep – you can measure this by dipping a plastic ruler or knife into the mixture; it will leave a mark showing the depth.

I like to weigh both halves to ensure I put the same amount of batter into each tin. This means they will both take the same amount of time to cook.

STEP 9 Bake for 30 minutes, then test the cakes with a skewer or small, sharp knife. You can always cook for a few minutes more, but you can't *unbake* them! They should appear well risen, but should still wobble a bit when shaken. There will be a crust on the top, which will sink back into the cake as it cools.

STEP 10 Remove from the oven and leave to cool in the tin. This sponge is fragile so remove it from the tin only when cool or it can break very easily.

See pages 61–63 for instructions on splitting and filling the cake.

Begin checking the bake after 30 minutes, and check periodically, as ovens vary greatly and the gauge of tin can also affect the cooking time.

SHELF LIFE AND STORAGE

This cake will keep at room temperature for a few days as long as it's well wrapped. Once iced, it will keep for 7–10 days. It also freezes well: wrap in baking parchment and foil, then seal in a freezer bag or wrap in cling film to prevent freezer burn. Freeze for up to 3 months.

RICH BELGIAN CHOCOLATE TRUFFLE CAKE QUANTITIES CHART

Here is a guide for the amounts of ingredients needed for different-sized tins. Remember that you always need two tins for each cake size. Bear in mind that square tins have a larger capacity than their round equivalent.

INGREDIENTS	15cm (6in) round	20cm (8in) round / 15cm (6in) square	25cm (10in) round / 20cm (8in) square	30cm (12in) square 25cm (10in) square
Plain 70% choc chips	240g	400g	560g	800g
Softened butter	300g	500g	700g	1kg
Soft light brown sugar	420g	700g	980g	1.4kg
Medium eggs, beaten	6	10	14	20
Vanilla extract	1 tsp	1 tsp	1½ tbsp	2 tbsp
Plain flour	240g	325g	460g	640g
160°C/ Gas mark 3	50 mins	1 hr	1 hr 30 mins	2 hrs

LEMON DRIZZLE SPONGE

A lemon cake is a perfect recipe for both celebrations and weddings and ideal when layered with zesty lemon buttercream (see recipe on page 50).
This is lovely in spring and summer, when you can accompany it with some fresh cream and raspberries if you want to serve it as a dessert. Using plenty of fresh lemon zest and the addition of the lively lemon syrup ensures a moist and delicious sponge. See the quantities chart overleaf for a guide to baking other sizes, if you want to make multiple tiers.

MAKES A 15CM (6IN) ROUND CAKE

For the lemon syrup
100ml caster sugar
100ml freshly squeezed lemon juice
  (from 6–7 lemons)
Grated zest of 2 lemons

For the lemon sponge
200g softened butter 100g golden caster sugar
100g soft light brown sugar
Grated zest of 3 lemons
4 medium eggs, lightly beaten
200g self-raising flour
Vanilla extract – as per chart page 39

Zest all the lemons first, before juicing them. You can save any zest that you aren't using by putting it into a freezer bag and freezing; you can re-use it straight from the freezer and mix into sponge batter, cookie dough or any other recipes that require it.

STEP 1 Preheat your oven to 180°C/Gas mark 4. Line a 15cm (6in) round cake tin with baking parchment (see page 19).

STEP 2 To make the syrup, mix the sugar and lemon juice in a pan and bring gently to the boil, stirring occasionally to prevent lumps or burning. Once it starts to boil, remove from the heat and allow to cool slightly. Alternatively, you can microwave this for a minute at a time on high power, stirring at each interval, until the sugar is completely dissolved and the syrup is really hot or boiling. Add the lemon zest and leave to infuse. Once cool, transfer to a squeezy bottle or jug for pouring.

STEP 3 For the sponge, beat the butter, both sugars and lemon zest together using a wooden spoon, hand mixer or electric mixer until the mixture is pale, soft and fluffy and the sugar granules have disappeared.

STEP 4 Add the beaten egg, a quarter at a time, mixing between each addition. If it curdles a little (looks lumpy and separated), just add a spoonful of flour from your weighed-out amount.

STEP 5 Now add the flour gradually, a quarter at a time, stirring it in gently as you go. Mix slowly, because if you mix it too quickly or over-process the flour, the sponge can turn out a bit chewy.

STEP 6 Spoon the cake mixture into your lined cake tin, pushing the mixture up the edges a bit, so that the sponge will rise high in the tin. Create a well in the centre – this will help your sponge to rise evenly and prevent a large hump from rising in the middle.

STEP 7 Bake for 30 minutes, then check –
you want a nice high sponge, and test with
a knife to be sure that the middle is cooked
through. You might need to cook it for
longer, even for up to an hour depending on
your oven. If you think the outside of the
cake is cooking too fast, turn the oven down
and cover the top of the cake with a piece
of foil to prevent it from burning.

STEP 8 When cooked, turn out onto a wire
rack and peel off the paper to allow the
steam to evaporate from the sponge. Whilst
the cake is still warm, spear through the
crust of your cake in several places with a
sharp knife or skewer and drizzle or brush
the sponge with the lemon syrup. To feed
the syrup into the holes you can use a
pastry brush or a squeezy sauce bottle or
drizzle it slowly from a jug with a spout.
You don't want it too soggy but you need
enough to soak in; it will take around 60ml
for this size of cake. Save the rest to use
in the middle of the cake when you later
split it to be filled. Leave the cake to
cool completely.

*See pages 61–63 for instructions on splitting and filling
the cake.*

SHELF LIFE AND STORAGE

Either use the cake straight away or store
by wrapping in plenty of cling film and
chilling for up to 3 days. You can also freeze
this cake for up to 3 months. Once iced,
it will keep well for up to 5 days if kept in
a cool, dry place.

The lemon syrup will keep in the fridge
for up to 2 weeks, and you can also freeze
it in small amounts. Just freeze portions
of around 100ml in small bags and get
them out to defrost the night before you
need them.

LEMON DRIZZLE CAKE QUANTITIES CHART

	15cm (6in) round	20cm (8in) round / 15cm (6in) square	25cm (10in) round / 20cm (8in) square	30cm (12in) square 25cm (10in) square	1-egg mix (for adding on larger amounts)
Softened butter	200g	400g	700g	1kg	50g
Golden caster sugar	100g	200g	350g	500g	25g
Soft light brown sugar	100g	200g	350g	500g	25g
Lemons, grated zest	3	6	10	15	1½
Medium eggs, beaten	4	8	14	20	1
Vanilla extract	1 tsp	2 tsp	1½ tbsp	2 tsp	¼ tsp
Self-raising flour	200g	400g	700g	1kg	50g
180°C/ Gas mark 4	30–40 mins	45 mins– 1 hr	1 hr 15 mins–1hr 30 mins	2 hrs – 2 hrs 30 mins	

One batch of the syrup will still be enough for all the above sizes of cake. Use the syrup to taste, brushing it over each layer of cake without soaking them. How much you need is really down to personal taste. Be careful, though; the cake can become sugary if too much syrup is used.

RICH BOOZY FRUIT CAKE

This divine recipe is perfect for celebrations. It's got loads of brandy in it and will keep for ages. See the quantities opposite for a guide to baking other sizes, if you want to make multiple tiers.

MAKES A 20CM (8IN) ROUND CAKE

300g natural-colour glacé cherries
480g raisins
540g currants
300g sultanas
60g mixed peel
240ml fine brandy, plus optional extra for brushing
240g softened butter
90g soft light brown sugar
180g molasses sugar
6 medium eggs, lightly beaten
300g plain flour
½ tsp ground cinnamon
½ tsp ground nutmeg
¼ tsp ground cloves
½ tsp ground ginger
½ tsp mixed spice
1 tsp vanilla extract

STEP 1 Wash the cherries well and cut them in half. Rinse the raisins, currants and sultanas in a sieve and drain thoroughly. Tip into a bowl, together with the cherries, then add the mixed peel and mix well. Pour the brandy over the mixture. Leave to soak overnight.

STEP 2 Preheat the oven to 160°C/Gas mark 3 and line a 20cm (8in) round cake tin with baking parchment (see page 19).

STEP 3 Melt the butter and sugars in the microwave, stirring every minute, until the butter has melted and the sugar and butter have become amalgamated. Alternatively, do this in a pan on a medium heat, stirring well to mix. Pour into a mixing bowl.

STEP 4 Add the beaten eggs to the sugar and butter. Stir with a wooden spoon.

STEP 5 In another bowl, place the flour and all the ground spices. Sift into another bowl to thoroughly combine the flour with the spices. Add the flour mixture to the wet sugar, butter and egg mixture.

STEP 6 Now stir in the steeped fruit and its remaining liquid, and the vanilla extract. Mix well, using your hands if it's easier.

STEP 7 Spoon the mixture into the prepared tin and bake for 2½ hours until a skewer inserted into the middle of the cake comes out clean. For an extra brandy kick, brush some brandy onto the top of the cake while it's still warm. Leave to cool in the tin.

STEP 8 When cool, turn the cake out of the tin and wrap in a double layer of greaseproof paper and a layer of foil, then store it until you are ready to decorate.

STORAGE AND SHELF LIFE

Ideally store this cake at room temperature for 5–6 weeks before covering it with marzipan or icing. It can be eaten earlier, but the flavour and intensity improve the longer it is stored. Covered in marzipan and icing, it will keep for a further 6 months at room temperature. Alternatively, freeze, wrapped in a double layer of greaseproof paper and a double layer of foil, then in a freezer bag, and it will last for ages.

RICH BOOZY FRUIT CAKE QUANTITIES CHART

The table below is a guide to the quantities needed for making your fruit cake in different sizes of tins. Note that some people find cloves overpowering, so if you aren't keen on them, take care not to add too much.

	15cm (6in) round	20cm (8in) round / 15cm (6in) square	25cm (10in) round / 20cm (8in) square	30cm (12in) square / 25cm (10in) square	30cm (12in) square
Natural-colour glacé cherries	200g	300g	400g	600g	800g
Raisins	320g	480g	640g	960g	1.28 kg
Currants	360g	540g	720g	1kg	1.44 kg
Sultanas	200g	300g	400g	600g	800g
Mixed peel	40g	60g	80g	120g	160g
Fine brandy	160ml	240ml	320ml	480ml	640ml
Softened butter	160g	240g	330g	480g	660g
Soft light brown sugar	60g	90g	130g	180g	260g
Molasses sugar	120g	180g	240g	360g	480g
Medium eggs, beaten	4	6	8	12	16
Plain flour	200g	300g	400g	600g	800g
Ground cinnamon	Just under ½ tsp	½ tsp	¾ tsp	1 tsp	3 tsp (1 tbsp)
Ground nutmeg	Just under ½ tsp	½ tsp	¾ tsp	1 tsp	3 tsp (1 tbsp)
Ground cloves	Just under ¼ tsp	¼ tsp	Scant ½ tsp	Just over ½ tsp	¾ tsp
Ground ginger	Just under ½ tsp	½ tsp	¾ tsp	1 tsp	3 tsp (1 tbsp)
Mixed spice	Just under ½ tsp	½ tsp	¾ tsp	1 tsp	3 tsp (1 tbsp)
Vanilla extract	1 tsp	1 tsp	1½ tsp	2 tsp	3 tsp (1 tbsp)
160°C/ Gas mark 3	Approx. 2 hrs	2 hrs 30 mins	3 hrs	3 hrs 30 mins	4 hrs

CHOCOLATE CUPCAKES

I have found that many chocolate cupcake recipes turn out really dry. While this recipe will obviously be heavier and denser than the vanilla cupcakes, my recipe has soured cream added, so is very moist. The cupcakes are deliciously chocolatey!

MAKES APPROX. 16 CUPCAKES

150g plain chocolate, 70% cocoa solids
  (chips or a broken-up bar)
150g softened butter
175g soft light brown sugar
2 eggs and 2 egg yolks
2 tbsp soured cream
1 tsp vanilla extract
125g self-raising flour
2 tbsp cocoa powder

STEP 1 Preheat the oven to 180°C/Gas mark 4. Take two 12-hole muffin trays and line 16 of the holes with paper muffin cases.

STEP 2 Melt the chocolate, butter and sugar together in a large heatproof bowl (make sure it's large, as you will eventually add everything else to this bowl, too). Ideally, do this in a microwave on medium heat for 1 minute at a time, stirring at each interval, until all melted together. Alternatively, place the bowl over a pan of simmering (not boiling) water until the chocolate is melted and the ingredients are amalgamated. Allow to cool slightly.

STEP 3 Whisk the whole eggs and yolks, soured cream and vanilla extract together in a separate bowl.

STEP 4 Sift the flour and cocoa into a bowl and mix with a spoon until combined.

STEP 5 Add the egg mixture to the melted chocolate mixture and stir together with a spoon until amalgamated.

STEP 6 Gently fold in the flour mixture until all the dry flour and cocoa has been incorporated into the wet ingredients.

STEP 7 Spoon into the paper cases, around half full. Bake for 15–20 minutes until just firm. Test with a sharp knife to ensure they are cooked through. Allow to cool for 5 minutes then turn out onto a wire rack. Once cool, decorate as required.

ZESTY ORANGE CUPCAKES

These gorgeous little sponges are delicious topped with dark-chocolate ganache (see page 54). They're a big hit at Christmas; the cakes taste like grown-up Jaffa cakes! The syrup quantities will make more than you need as it will cover about 30 cupcakes, but you can't make it much smaller. You can store leftovers in the fridge for up to a week, or it freezes very well; pour it into little freezer bags and get it out as and when you need. Alternatively, if you are baking loads, just increase the recipe as needed.

MAKES 12–16 CUPCAKES

For the orange syrup
100ml sugar
100ml freshly squeezed orange juice
   (from about 6 oranges; zest 4 of them first)
Grated zest of 2 oranges (saved from above)
1 tbsp orange liqueur, such as Cointreau
   or Grand Marnier (optional)

For the orange sponge
200g softened butter
100g golden caster sugar
100g soft light brown sugar
Grated zest of 2 oranges (saved from the syrup)
4 medium eggs, lightly beaten
200g self-raising flour

STEP 1 Preheat your oven to 200°C/Gas mark 4. Line one or two 12-hole muffin trays with paper muffin cases.

STEP 2 Mix the sugar and orange juice in a pan and bring gently to the boil, stirring occasionally to dissolve lumps.

Alternatively, you can microwave for 1 minute at a time until all the sugar crystals have dissolved and the syrup has boiled. Once it starts to boil, remove from the heat. Add the orange zest and leave to infuse. Once cool, stir in the liqueur, if using, then transfer the syrup to a squeezy bottle or jug for pouring.

STEP 3 For the sponge, combine the butter, both types of sugar and the orange zest and beat, with a wooden spoon, hand mixer or in an electric mixer on medium–fast speed, until the mixture is very pale, soft and fluffy and the sugar granules have disappeared.

STEP 4 Add the beaten eggs, a quarter at a time, and mix in slowly at each addition. If it curdles a little (looks lumpy and separated) just add a spoonful of flour from your weighed-out amount.

STEP 5 Now add the flour gradually, a quarter at a time, gently stirring it in as you go. Mix slowly, because if you mix it quickly and over-process the flour, the sponge can turn out a bit chewy.

STEP 6 Divide the mixture between the paper cases and cook for 10–15 minutes. Check after 10 minutes, as all ovens vary. When done, the cakes should be a light golden brown and springy to the touch; if you want to be sure, test with a sharp knife. This should come out clean and free of mixture if the cakes are cooked through.

STEP 7 Once they are baked, turn the cakes out onto a wire rack. Use a pastry brush to coat the tops with a little of the orange syrup, or use a squeezy bottle to squirt it on – or pour from a jug. Leave to cool, then decorate the cupcakes as required.

BASIC VANILLA COOKIES

This recipe is so easy; you just make the dough and roll it out, then cut out any shape you wish. I use this to make lovely cookies for treats, presents, party or wedding favours, as well as cake decorations (see page 217 for the Cookie Explosion cake). You can also use this recipe to create cookie 'lollipops' by baking with a stick embedded into the dough. I give these as gifts and treats, and use them on top of the Cookie Explosion cake. If you want to spice things up a bit, you can change the flavourings in this mixture. For example, if you want orange or lemon cookies, instead of vanilla, you can use the grated zest of two oranges or two lemons. To make them chocolatey, replace 25g of the plain flour with 25g cocoa powder.

MAKES APPROX. 20 MEDIUM COOKIES
200g softened butter
150g golden caster sugar
50g soft light brown sugar
Seeds scraped from 1 vanilla pod
1 medium egg, lightly beaten
200g plain flour, plus extra for dusting

EQUIPMENT:
20 lolly/cookie sticks (optional)

STEP 1 Preheat the oven to 190°C/Gas mark 5 and line two baking sheets with baking parchment. Mix the butter and both types of sugar with the vanilla seeds (or orange or lemon zest if you prefer) until just combined but still grainy. Do NOT cream like you would for a sponge mix or you may find your cookies spread, puff up a bit and lose their shape definition. Either do this with a wooden spoon, hand mixer or in a electric mixer on a slow speed. If using an electric mixer, you may need to pause it a couple of times and scrape the mixture down into the centre of the bowl before continuing, to totally incorporate the butter.

STEP 2 Add the egg, a little at a time, mixing in each addition with a wooden spoon or with your mixer on slow. Repeat until all the egg is mixed in.

STEP 3 Add the flour to your mixture and mix slowly until a dough forms. If you like, you can do this with your hands. If your dough is still a bit sticky you might need to add a little more flour, or if it's dry, add a tiny bit more beaten egg. You need it to be firm and easy to roll out without sticking to your rolling pin.

STEP 4 Dust your worktop with plenty of flour and roll out the cookie dough. Work from the centre, rolling away from your body, then from the centre towards you. Keep turning the dough a quarter-turn. This will help you to roll out a uniform oblong as opposed to a spidery shape, which is more difficult to cut shapes from. Take care to apply even pressure, and roll to an approximate thickness of 5mm. If you have guide sticks, use them to ensure you get an even thickness and that the cookies all bake evenly.

STEP 5 Now cut out your required shapes with a cookie cutter(s). Alternatively, you can draw or print out a shape, glue it onto card and cut around it with scissors. Place this template onto the top of the dough and cut around the shape with a sharp knife. You might need to gently smooth any jagged edges with your fingertips to make them look neat.

STEP 6 With a palette knife or very careful fingers, place your cookies on the prepared baking sheets. At this point, if you want to add sticks to the cookies, simply push a stick gently into the dough, to about half way, with the fingers of your other hand pressing gently onto the point where you are inserting it, to prevent the dough from breaking. It takes a bit of practice, but you can always re-roll the dough if it goes wrong.

STEP 7 Bake for around 10–12 minutes. Check after 10 minutes; you may need to give them a few more minutes. The cookies should be golden brown, firm and springy to touch but not too dark. Cool on a wire rack and then decorate as required.

For ideas of how to decorate or cover your cookies, see pages 129–132.

If you bake the cookies until they are very dry, they will last longer. You can give them 10–20 minutes extra but do this at a lower temperature so that they properly dry out and don't burn — turn the oven down by 10–20°C.

FILLINGS
AND
COVERINGS

CHAPTER
2

VANILLA BEAN BUTTERCREAM AND VARIATIONS

A simple buttercream is really quite easy to make, and I recommend that you use the best possible ingredients. If you can, use natural unbleached icing sugar, which has a lovely golden quality (only use this inside cakes, though, if you need a whiter finish for covering a cake), and use a good-quality unsalted butter, ideally organic. It also makes a difference how you whip the buttercream, to make sure that it is super-smooth and creamy. Buttercream is a perfect filling for celebration or wedding cakes. Indeed, you can even use it for cupcakes (although I give a slightly lighter buttercream recipe for cupcakes on page 51). Increase the quantities of this recipe as needed, and like most of the cakes and fillings, you can freeze any that is left over. Once you have this basic buttercream, you can use it as the base for many delicious flavours; see the variations below. (The buttercream in the picture is the Fresh Raspberry and Strawberry recipe on page 50.) Bear in mind that if you are making a cake with a few tiers, you can make one large batch of vanilla buttercream, then divide it into portions, each to be flavoured differently if required.

FILLS AND COVERS A 20CM (8IN) ROUND CAKE

Makes approx. 750g

250g soft unsalted butter

500g sifted icing sugar (use the natural, unbleached one inside cakes if you can get it; for covering cakes, use a bright white icing sugar)

2 tsp vanilla extract

1 vanilla pod, seeds scraped out (save the pod for syrups or put in your sugar jar to infuse)

STEP 1 In an electric mixer with the beater or paddle attachment (or in a bowl using a hand mixer or wooden spoon), cream the butter with the vanilla seeds and extract until pale, soft and smooth.

STEP 2 Add about a quarter of the icing sugar. Mix to combine, slowly at first so that the sugar doesn't puff up all over your kitchen. Once it is all mixed in, beat for about 30 seconds on fast until the mixture is really creamy and pale. It will take a few minutes if mixing by hand.

STEP 3 Continue adding the sugar in quarter increments, taking care to completely beat it in after each addition.

STEP 4 Finally, beat the buttercream on fast for a minute or two until it's fluffy and pale. You can now use the buttercream, colour it or adapt into many different flavours.

COLOURING BUTTERCREAM

You can tint or colour buttercream using liquid or paste food colourings. If using a liquid colour, bear in mind that adding too much liquid may give a sloppy buttercream, so if you want a very strong colour I recommend using a strong professional food-colouring paste. Once the colouring is added, either beat in an electric mixer (this is the quickest and easiest method) or take the required amount into a bowl and beat with a wooden spoon.

See pages 86–88 for using the buttercream as a covering on your cake.

ORANGE BUTTERCREAM

Follow the basic vanilla buttercream recipe (see page 49), but when you cream the butter, add the grated zest of 2 fresh oranges. (You can still include the vanilla, if you wish, or you can omit it if you prefer.) The zest will infuse into the buttercream to make a delicious orange-flavoured filling.

LEMON BUTTERCREAM

Again, using vanilla buttercream as a base, you can turn it into a gorgeous lemon filling. Follow the vanilla recipe then add the grated zest of two lemons, along with 200g lemon curd. (You can use homemade curd, or there are plenty of great-quality ready-made brands available — being an Essex girl I'm a fan of the Tiptree one, it is lovely and tangy.) Stir these into the buttercream after you've added the icing sugar, until combined, and you have a perfect accompaniment to your lemon sponge.

FRESH RASPBERRY AND STRAWBERRY BUTTERCREAM

For a fresh raspberry kick and the summery taste of strawberries, add 4 tablespoons of the following fruit coulis to the basic vanilla buttercream (see page 49). You can then use as you wish to fill any cakes. A great combination is to split a vanilla sponge twice and add one layer of vanilla buttercream and another layer of the berry buttercream — not only does this look really appealing when cut, but it tastes divine!

STEP 1 Take a small punnet each of fresh raspberries and strawberries (approximately 200–250g of each), rinse the fruit and put into a food processor or use a hand blender to purée. (Alternatively you can use a potato masher to mash the fruit in a bowl.) Pass the purée through a sieve into a small pan.

STEP 2 Place the pan on a low heat and bring the purée to a gentle boil, then leave to cool. Or you can use a microwave for this stage.

STEP 3 Add approximately 4 tablespoons of the cooled fruity paste to the vanilla buttercream and mix well.

BELGIAN CHOCOLATE GANACHE BUTTERCREAM

This will give you a perfect chocolate buttercream that's ideal for filling the Belgian Chocolate Truffle Cake (see page 35) or even the Very Vanilla Sponge (see page 31) if you like. It can also be used as a cake covering. Once again, start with the vanilla buttercream recipe on page 49. As always, you can increase the quantities by doubling, etc.

STEP 1 Put 200g fresh double cream and 400g good-quality plain Belgian chocolate (minimum 70% cocoa solids – either chips or a bar broken into small chunks) into a microwave-proof bowl and heat on medium power for a minute at a time, stirring periodically, until the chocolate has melted into the cream to form a smooth, velvety ganache. Alternatively, you can do this in a heatproof bowl over a pan of gently simmering water until you achieve the same melted result. Leave to cool.

STEP 2 Once cooled, stir the ganache into the buttercream. Be sure that it's completely cool, as warm chocolate will make your buttercream oily and unusable!

CUPCAKE BUTTERCREAM

When icing and decorating cupcakes, I used to find that if I topped them with buttercream, the next day they would go a bit crunchy, and the buttercream would crystallise on top. So I tried out ways to combat this problem and discovered a way to prevent it.

To prolong the life of your buttercream and keep it soft for longer, add a quantity of cream cheese to it. This makes it taste lovely too. Once again, begin with the vanilla buttercream on page 49, then add 150g cream cheese, a good-quality one, slowly beating it into the finished buttercream. You can then flavour the buttercream as normal. This is ideal for cupcake covering, but can also be used to decorate a whole cake.

If you are making it in advance, keep the buttercream in the fridge for up to a week. Make sure to get it out and leave at room temperature for a couple of hours before use.

ROYAL ICING

Once you have mastered this recipe it will be a loyal friend to you in your cake-decorating quest. We use it every day at Fancy Nancy, for piping messages, trims, borders and patterns, covering cakes or making run-out decorations (see pages 129–132) to go on cakes and cookies. We also use it for sticking cake tiers together, attaching decorations and images, filling gaps and even for covering up mistakes. It's invaluable.

This recipe makes enough royal icing to decorate around 20 cookies if you are using several colours for the designs. In each icing bag you will need at least 100g (any smaller and it's tricky to pipe with), so you will probably have some left over. If so, it can be stored in an airtight container or food bag for up to a week. You can also multiply this recipe to make larger amounts if you are making more than 20 cookies or creating larger cakes.

You can also buy ready-made royal-icing mix from most supermarkets; you just add water to it. It works well on cookies and can be coloured and used in the same way described here.

MAKES APPROX. 600G ROYAL ICING
500g sifted icing sugar
2 medium egg whites
Juice of 2 lemons

STEP 1 Place the icing sugar in a large bowl or use an electric mixer with the paddle attachment. Add the egg whites and whisk by hand or run the machine on its slowest speed to start mixing them in. Once it starts to amalgamate, add the lemon juice, then mix by hand or on the slowest speed for 5 minutes.

STEP 2 Adjust the icing to the consistency that you need, by adding more icing sugar or liquid. See page 126 for more details on how to achieve stiff-peak, soft-peak or runny consistencies of royal icing.

STEP 3 Once ready, cover the bowl with a clean, damp tea towel or cloth, to keep the icing from going hard. If exposed to the air, it will begin to skin over after just a few minutes. This is not good; even if you stir the flaky bits in, they always block up your piping nozzle.

See page 82 for using royal icing as a covering on your cake.

FONDANT ICING

Although you can make fondant icing yourself, there are also some amazing ready-made products available that work really well. You simply add hot water to these. I like to use Tate & Lyle fondant icing sugar; it's quick and has a good finish. You can also buy good-quality fondant from specialist stores, including suppliers like Squires Kitchen; you can order online, theirs is a particularly good one. If you wish, you can flavour your fondant icing with oils or essences such as vanilla, orange and rose water — I have even been known to add a dash of Absinth!

COVERS 12–16 LARGE CUPCAKES
500g pack of fondant icing sugar
Hot water (boiled then cooled slightly)
Paste or liquid colours (optional)

STEP 1 Pour the fondant icing sugar into a bowl and add a few splashes of hot water. Take care: you want it to be *just* the right consistency, not so runny that it won't set, and not so stiff that it won't drop off the spoon. You are looking for a treacle-like consistency, so that it clings to the spoon but will still drop off. Stir slowly and smoothly until you reach the right consistency, have eliminated all the dry sugary bits and are left with a smooth fondant. Avoid using a whisking motion or you will get too many bubbles in the fondant, which can spoil the finish of your cakes.

STEP 2 If you want to add colour, add a tiny dab of the paste or liquid to the fondant. I like to use the lightest colours first, as you can sometimes change these into new colours without having to wash the bowl out. Save time wherever you can.

See page 96 for using fondant icing as a covering on your cupcakes.

GLOSSY CHOCOLATE GANACHE FOR POURING

STORAGE AND SHELF LIFE

Leftover ganache can be re-used on another cake or put into a piping bag and used to decorate any cakes. It can be stored in a plastic container in the fridge for up to 2 weeks, or it freezes well too; just make sure you defrost it in the fridge overnight. It can then be gently heated to reach its liquid pouring consistency again.

This smooth, silky, rich chocolate ganache recipe is so simple, and perfect for pouring over a whole celebration cake or for using to top cupcakes. It's a perfect marriage with Zesty Orange Cupcakes (see page 43), especially at Christmas!

COVERS A 15CM (6IN) ROUND CAKE OR 12–16 CUPCAKES

300g chocolate chips or broken-up chocolate, 70% cocoa solids
125g unsalted butter
90ml double cream

STEP 1 Place all the ingredients together in a microwave-proof bowl and microwave on medium for 1 minute. Stir the mixture, then put back in the microwave and repeat the process until all the ingredients are melted together. Alternatively, you can place all the ingredients in a pan and heat gently, stirring often, until melted together.

STEP 2 Leave to cool slightly. The ganache is now ready to use (see page 99).

DARK BELGIAN CHOCOLATE PASTE

This chocolate coating can also be referred to as roll-out chocolate, modelling chocolate, moulding chocolate, cocoform or chocolate plastique. When looking to buy this ready-made, be aware that brands may describe it and name it differently. However, I refer to it throughout this book as chocolate paste. It is very easy to make and great for covering cakes as it looks really luxurious and suits all manner of occasions. I particularly like adding metallic-effect lustres to this for a gorgeous finish. If you want to make a milk chocolate coating, you can just mix together equal quantities of this and the white chocolate coating (see page 56). This recipe will cover a 20cm (8in) round cake with excess that you can use for making models or flowers, or freeze for another time. If you are making a larger tiered cake, multiply the recipe accordingly.

COVERS A 20CM (8IN) ROUND CAKE

750g good-quality Belgian chocolate – chips or a broken-up bar (not strong 70% chocolate or else the coating won't set; 50–55% cocoa solids are better here)

550g liquid glucose (or golden syrup if you can't get it)

EQUIPMENT:
Kitchen thermometer

STEP 1 Put the chocolate in a large microwave-proof bowl and melt in the microwave on medium power, for a minute at a time, stirring at each interval. Alternatively, melt the chocolate in a heatproof bowl set over a pan of just-simmering water until smooth and melted. Heat the chocolate to around 40°C – check with a thermometer.

STEP 2 In a small pan, gently heat the glucose syrup or golden syrup separately, also to 40°C, so that the two mixtures are at the same temperature.

STEP 3 Pour the syrup onto the melted chocolate and stir vigorously until thoroughly amalgamated.

STEP 4 With the mixture still in its warm, viscous state, pour it carefully into a large, heavy-duty freezer bag. You might need help with this, or you can place the bag in a bowl or pan with the top of the bag rolled over the sides to keep it open, to avoid any spillage. Leave to cool overnight at room temperature. It will set into a paste that can then be kneaded until pliable and used in the same way as sugarpaste or marzipan.

STEP 5 If you will be decorating your entire cake with moulded chocolate ruffles, flowers etc., just one coat of this paste will suffice. But if you wish to have lots of the coated surface on show, I recommend two layers of this covering for the cake to look its best.

See page 103 for using the chocolate coating as a covering on your cake.

WHITE BELGIAN CHOCOLATE PASTE

This amount covers a 20cm (8in) round cake and you will probably have some left over that you can re-use. It keeps well at room temperature, wrapped up in a food bag, for up to 2 weeks and it freezes for up to 3 months. If you are making a larger tiered cake, you can multiply the recipe accordingly. To begin with, you need to make a sugar syrup. The syrup recipe makes double what you need, but it's hard to make it in a smaller quantity. Just freeze whatever you don't use; it will keep for up to 3 months.

COVERS A 20CM (8IN) ROUND CAKE

900g good-quality white Belgian chocolate –
  chips or a broken-up bar
60g cocoa butter
200g glucose syrup (or golden syrup if you can't
  get it – your coating will be a darker colour)

For the sugar syrup

150g golden caster sugar
50g liquid glucose
200ml water

STEP 1 To make the sugar syrup, place the ingredients in a microwave-proof bowl and bring to the boil by microwaving on high for a minute at a time and stirring at each interval. Alternatively, bring gently to the boil on the hob in a small pan. Leave to cool slightly.

STEP 2 Put the chocolate in a large microwave-proof bowl and melt in the microwave on medium power, just for a minute at a time, stirring at each interval. Alternatively, melt in a heatproof bowl set over a pan of just-simmering water until smooth and melted.

STEP 3 Melt the cocoa butter in a microwave-proof bowl in the microwave until liquid or again do this on the hob in a heatproof bowl sat over simmering water.

STEP 4 Pour the liquid cocoa butter into the melted white chocolate and stir gently until thoroughly amalgamated.

STEP 5 Place 150ml of the sugar syrup into a microwave-proof bowl, add the glucose or golden syrup and warm for a minute or two until they become fully incorporated together. This is easiest in a microwave on medium power, but you can also melt them together in a heatproof bowl over a pan of just-simmering (not boiling) water, Don't allow the mixture to get too hot – it should be no hotter than body temperature, so keep checking it – as when you pour it into the chocolate in the next step there shouldn't be a great difference in temperature between the two.

STEP 6 Pour the syrup mixture into the large bowl of melted chocolate and work these together using a wooden spoon with a fast, deep, beating motion. You need to work it quickly to avoid ending up with any lumps of unmixed chocolate or cocoa butter in your final cooled coating.

STEP 7 Now, while the coating is still in its warm, viscous state, pour it carefully into a large, heavy-duty freezer bag. You might need help with this, or you can place the bag in a bowl or pan with the top of the bag rolled over the sides to keep it open, to avoid any mishaps.

STEP 8 Leave to cool overnight. It will set into a paste that can then be kneaded until pliable and used in the same way as sugarpaste or marzipan.

STEP 9 If you will be decorating your entire cake with moulded chocolate ruffles, flowers etc., just one coat of this paste will suffice. But if you wish to have lots of the coated surface on show, I recommend two layers of this covering for the cake to look its best.

See page 103 for using the chocolate coating as a covering on your cake.

LAYERING
AND
CONSTRUCTING
CAKES

CHAPTER
3

Once your lovely sponge cake is baked to perfection,
you can now fill it with some delicious buttercream (see
page 49) chocolate ganache (see page 51) or anything else
that takes your fancy. This will bring your sponge to life!
The sponge and filling recipes I've given in this book are
tried and tested at Fancy Nancy, and work really well for
cake decorating. You can mix them up in any way you like
or, of course, you can use other recipes in countless
different flavours. Everyone has their favourites!

The fillings and layering methods in this chapter can
be used not only to add flavour, but also to fill any holes,
lumps or bumps in your sponge. This is so you end up
with a perfectly smooth base coating, which will make
for the best finish possible. I'll explain some tricks
I've learned along the way to make sure you have a great
base to start your decorating. A good foundation is half
the battle in the quest for cake perfection and it
will really save you time in the long run.

LAYERING THE VERY VANILLA AND LEMON DRIZZLE SPONGES

So, you've made your sponge, baked it a bit higher than your tin and achieved a nice flat top by popping the sponge back in the tin and slicing off the excess. Now it's time to split the cake and fill it, to create a sound foundation for decorating. It is well worth spending the time at this point to get the base sponge right. I know you want to whizz along to the fun bit of decorating, but if you start with a great base, your finished product will look extra special and you'll be glad that you took your time.

For layering the Very Vanilla sponge, I like to slice it twice and fill it with two layers of buttercream, one of Vanilla Bean Buttercream (see page 49), and another of Fresh Raspberry and Strawberry Buttercream (see page 50), as this tastes delicious and the two layers look really pretty when the cake is cut. Of course, you don't have to do this if you don't want to or are in a hurry. You can simply split it once and layer with whatever filling you fancy. For the Lemon Drizzle cake, you only need to split it once. You'll need approximately one batch (750g) of buttercream for layering a 20cm (8in) round cake.

If you do a lot of cake decorating, you might want to invest in a cake leveller; I swear by mine for this task. With this really handy tool, I just measure the depth I need and then slice away; it cuts off the top and leaves you with a perfectly level cake on which to work.

Sticking the cake to the board stops it from sliding about when you add marzipan and icing, which would make the job very tricky and probably result in a bad finish.

STEP 1 When you slice a cake, no matter how precisely you measure it, or even if you use a cake leveller for cutting, there will always be slight undulations in the sponge, so sometimes when you sandwich it back together again, the two halves don't fit back in exactly the same position and you end up with a slightly wonky cake! My dad, George, came up with a great idea to help with this: before you slice the cake, take a serrated knife and score a line all the way down one edge of your cake so that you can line it back up again when you put the two halves back together. Now, when you split your cake, even if you go a bit wonky, you will be able to fit it back together in exactly the right place, like a jigsaw, using the line as a guide.

STEP 2 Cut little marks into the sponge around the edge of your cake, measured out with a ruler at 5cm (2in) intervals to indicate the line to which you will slice through. Mark roughly in the centre for the Lemon Drizzle (page 37) or a single-layer Very Vanilla cake (page 31). If you're using two layers of filling, mark roughly one-third and two-thirds up the sponge. If you have a cake leveller, set it in the centre for one layer, or at a 2.5cm (1in) depth then at a 5cm (2in) depth for two layers. Then slice right across your sponge once or twice.

STEP 3 At this stage, I like to add a little drizzle of syrup to the cut side of the cake so it can soak into the sponge before adding your filling and sandwiching together. Apply the syrup with a pastry brush or trickle it from a jug; you don't want the cake to become soggy so apply just enough to keep the cake nice and moist. The syrup will also extend its shelf life. (If you followed my cake recipes, you should have some sugar syrup left over for this. If you used a different cake recipe, see page 31 and 37 for how to make sugar syrups.)

STEP 4 Now you need to adhere the bottom portion of your sliced sponge cake to a cake board the same size as the cake. I find that a large splodge of buttercream directly onto the board is the best way to stick on the cake and prevent it from sliding around.

STEP 5 Next, spread a generous layer of your chosen buttercream over the top of the base sponge cake as evenly as possible with a palette knife.

STEP 6 If you have only sliced the cake once, take the top piece (again you can drizzle the cut side of this too if you wish with some syrup) and invert over the layer of buttercream filling, lining up your guiding knife mark. (If you are doing two layers of filling, place the middle piece of sponge on top of the bottom, line up the knife mark, then drizzle over a little more syrup and top with the next layer of filling. Place the top piece of sponge over the middle piece, again using the knife mark as a guide, so that you have a perfectly level and even cake.)

STEP 7 Once your sponge is filled and sandwiched together, you can smooth over with more buttercream, or you can simply brush with jam and add icing straight onto the sponge, but it does look better if you give it a smooth buttercream covering first.

LAYERING THE RICH BELGIAN CHOCOLATE TRUFFLE CAKE

As mentioned in the recipe on page 35, my chocolate sponge is baked in two halves. I love to sandwich it with the Belgian Chocolate Ganache Buttercream (see page 51) — they are a perfect marriage. It's not imperative to do the outer buttercream layer if you don't have the tools or the time, but it does make for a nice cake and finish. If you wish, you can simply brush the cake with jam and add icing or marzipan straight onto the sponge without the buttercream layer. Or you can use it to make one of the spectacular ganache cakes (see pages 190–3).

STEP 1 To layer your chocolate sponge with buttercream, you first need to turn your cakes out of their tins. This sponge is a fairly dense, crumbly one, with a crust on the top, almost like a brownie, so it's best to either use a wire rack or a cake board that's larger than the tin. Place this over the top of the tin, then carefully invert, so that your sponge is left with the bottom facing upwards.

STEP 2 Leave the cakes with the base parchment on and then turn them back over by placing another wire rack or cake board on the up-facing base of the cake, then carefully flipping over again so that the crust is now on top.

STEP 3 Carefully slice the top crust off each sponge. As a general guide, I like to work on cakes with an 8cm (3in) depth, so ideally you should measure 4cm (1 ½in) up the side of each cake and slice off at this point. (You can use a normal ruler for this, and mark all around the edge at intervals of about 5cms. This will help to ensure that you don't cut the sponge off at a wonky angle.)

When layering your cakes, use the top, cut edge as the bottom of the cake and use the bottom of the sponge (the bit that was in the tin) as the top. This will give you a firm, smooth surface rather than a crumbly surface.

STEP 4 Once both halves are ready, take the appropriate-sized cake board (for example, a 15cm (6in) sponge needs to go on a 15cm (6in) cake board) and spread a little of your chosen buttercream or filling onto the board to help the sponge to stick.

STEP 5 Now spread a good layer of the buttercream or filling evenly over the cut top surface of the base half. It's easiest to do this with a palette knife, if you have one, otherwise a regular knife will do. Try to achieve a layer of buttercream that is approximately 2mm deep, no more, as you want enough to make the cake taste great, but not so much that the filling forces itself out at the sides.

STEP 6 Take the other half of your sponge and carefully invert over the bottom cake, so that both cut sides are facing each other in the middle and the top of your cake is the nice straight-edged base of that half.

STEP 7 Once you have these sandwiched together, if you want to be very fussy about the straightness and levelness of the cake (important if you are making a stacked design), it's a good idea not only to check by eye but also to use a spirit level. You can buy a small, cheap spirit level from most DIY stores and even some supermarkets. The best way to test is to place a cake board on the top surface of the sponge and sit the spirit level on top of the cake board. If you

can see that it's slightly higher on one side, this is usually because the filling is uneven (assuming you have cut the sponge level, of course!), so you can simply push down where you need to until the spirit level reading is central.

STEP 8 Once you have a level sponge, take a palette knife all the way around the edge of your cake to smooth off the filling.

STEP 9 From this point on, I like to work with the cake on a large round cake board that's 5–8cm (2–3in) wider than the cake on its base board. This is easier than working directly onto a worktop or, especially, a turntable, because when you are spreading buttercream, etc. around the sides, the cake board will prevent any mess from going onto your turntable or worktop. Working on a board also aids spreading and covering, as it allows you to easily spin the cake round using the board underneath.

STEP 10 You can now ice the cake as it is, or you can add an entire layer of thin buttercream to the outside if you wish – it makes the chocolate sponge taste wonderful. To do this, take a splodge of buttercream on your palette knife and spread it all around the sides of your cake. Also spread a layer of buttercream over the top, making sure the surface is completely covered and there are no holes where the sponge is still showing. You don't want a thick coating; just a thin all-over spreading of buttercream (a scraping is enough).

STEP 11 If you have a side scraper, you can now use this to scrape off excess buttercream, leaving you with a perfectly straight, thin, smooth coating. Hold the side scraper at a 90-degree angle to the cake board and facing in towards the cake, at about a 30–45-degree angle to the surface. Rotate the cake whilst pulling the scraper towards you. If you don't have a side scraper, you can use a small 15cm (6in)plastic ruler – a wider one works best. Its straight, flat edges do the job pretty well.

STEP 12 For the top of the cake, scrape off the excess using a straight edge tool (a ruler-type tool that is used for royal icing. If you don't have one, you can improvise with the straight side of a long bread knife – be careful of your fingers! – or use a regular 30cm/12in plastic ruler). Bend down so that your eyes are level with the top of the cake, then drag the buttercream from the back of the cake towards you, holding the tool at a 45-degree angle. This will leave a smooth top.

LEVELLING THE RICH
BOOZY FRUIT CAKE

This is the easiest cake to construct, as although the recipe and method is more involved, there is no splitting and filling to do, so you can get pretty much straight on with the covering stage.

As with the other sponges, use the top baked edge of the sponge as the bottom. Invert it over the cake board to reveal the flat, bottom part of the fruit cake, which will be smoother and more level as the top of your cake.

It's useful to stick the fruit cake to the correct-sized board by brushing with a little boiled jam and a sticking a few small pieces of marzipan to the board to prevent the fruit cake from sliding around when you come to cover it.

However, if your fruit cake isn't quite level or has any holes in the edges etc., it's a good idea to sort all this out before you start covering, so that when you add marzipan or icing, you won't get any lumps or bumps.

You need to get the sides and top as square as possible to get the best finish. If you have any holes in the sides of your cake, plug them with marzipan. Also, fruit cakes sometimes shrink a bit, so when you invert the sponge to get the flat base on top, there might be a gap around the bottom. Fill this with a sausage of marzipan or sugarpaste, going all around the base, so that when you ice the cake, the covering will sit nice and flush with your base board, and you won't be left with an unsightly indent in your finished cake.

If the top of the fruit cake is not level, you can build up the dips with marzipan. Roll out a piece of marzipan to the approximate thickness, then, by eye, cut out a patch of marzipan to place onto the dipped part, building up the top until it is flat. It's a bit tricky and might take several minutes but if you want your covering to be even it's worth doing this at the base level.

ICING CAKES

CHAPTER 4

DECISIONS FIRST – WHAT TO USE TO COVER YOUR CAKES AND CUPCAKES?

Now that you are ready to cover your cake, there are so many different ways in which to do this. So how do you make your decision? All coatings and coverings have different tastes and looks, but you need to consider which is most appropriate for the design you want to give your cake creation. For example, you can't hand-paint onto a glossy chocolate ganache surface, royal icing or buttercream.

Sugarpaste is the best and most commonly used covering because you can apply every different cake-decorating method and technique to it. It's a fabulous product that comes in white, ivory and an array of colours (or you can colour your own) and gives you a smooth and even surface. You can pipe onto it, add sugar models, embellishments or pictures to it, or even cake-jazzle it (see page 199)! Usually, large cakes are first covered with a layer of marzipan then left for a day before being covered with sugarpaste.

You can also use liquid icings that set on the cake, including classic royal icing (see page 52), chocolate ganache (see page 54) and fondant icing (see page 53), which you can also buy easily in the supermarket – you simply add boiled water to it and it's excellent to work with.

Covering a cake with chocolate is also a lovely idea because, as well as being simple, it tastes really delicious. There are a few ways of doing this: they all have different looks and you should bear in mind that some chocolate-covered cakes cannot be decorated as intricately as an iced cake. If you wish to decorate, paint or embellish a chocolate cake, Belgian chocolate paste gives a smooth surface and is used in the same way as sugarpaste. You need to remember, however, that if it is a dark colour, some other colours or hand-painted designs won't stand out as well as on plain sugarpaste. You can buy Belgian chocolate paste coating fairly easily (see stockists on page 234, but don't confuse it with chocolate-flavoured icing, which has a horrible artificial taste!) or you can make your own; it's relatively easy and tastes wonderful – see the recipe on page 55.

This chapter also includes extra tips for each type of cake covering, e.g. practising on a cake board, finishing royal icing, etc.

COVERING WITH MARZIPAN AND SUGARPASTE

To cover a cake in the traditional way, a layer of marzipan is applied to the cake first, followed by a layer of sugarpaste. It is always best to give cakes two layers of covering, as this not only preserves your cake better but helps to achieve a smoother, more flawless surface on which to decorate.

Marzipan is an excellent medium for the first layer, as it holds in all the lovely moistness due to its high oil content. Do remember, however, that you can't use it if someone has a nut allergy, as it contains almonds. In this case, use a thicker coating of sugarpaste, or for a much better finish, I recommend using two layers of sugarpaste.

The charts below give a guide to the amounts of marzipan and sugarpaste needed for covering different-sized cakes. It does takes a bit of trial and error to get to know the exact amount of marzipan you need, but I think it's best to roll out a bit too much to be on the safe side; you can easily re-use the excess. So these quantities allow enough for you to cover your cake and still have some room to play; cut off the excess as soon as you've laid it over the cake, and pop it in a food bag to keep it fresh.

Cake Size	15cm (6in) round	15cm (6in) square	20cm (8in) round	20cm (8in) square	25cm (10in) round	25cm (10in) square
Marzipan	650g	800g	850g	1kg	1.2kg	1.5kg
Cake Size	30cm (12in) round	30cm (12in) square	35cm (14in) round	35cm (14in) square	40cm (16in) round	40cm (16in) square
Marzipan	1.5kg	1.75kg	1.75kg	2kg	2.5kg	3kg
Cake Size	15cm (6in) round	15cm (6in) square	20cm (8in) round	20cm (8in) square	25cm (10in) round	25cm (10in) square
Sugarpaste	700g	900g	1kg	1.25kg	1.25kg	1.65kg
Cake Size	30cm (12in) round	30cm (12in) square	35cm (14in) round	35cm (14in) square	40cm (16in) round	40cm (16in) square
Sugarpaste	1.75kg	2.25kg	2.4kg	2.9kg	2.9kg	3.5kg

FIRST COAT:
MARZIPAN

If you have decided not to use marzipan, because of an allergy or if you just don't like it, you can apply an initial layer of sugarpaste to your cake instead, in exactly the same way as described here. Then, the next day, apply a second sugarpaste coat as described on page 77.

You will need:
A cake, split and filled and adhered to a base
    board with buttercream
Apricot jam
Icing sugar
Marzipan (see chart on page 71 for amount)

Equipment:
Greaseproof paper
Pastry brush
Plastic icing rolling pin
Guide sticks (optional)
Top smoother (optional)
2 side smoothers (optional)
Small, sharp knife
Pin tool or pin
Turntable
Cake board, 5–8cm (2–3in) larger than the cake

(See the step-by-step photographs, overleaf)

STEP 1 The surface of the cake needs to be sticky so that the marzipan will adhere to it; I use apricot jam for this. Microwave the jam for a couple of minutes until boiling (this is to ensure that no bacteria becomes trapped between the cake and the marzipan). If you don't have a microwave, bring the jam to the boil in a pan on the hob.

STEP 2 Place the cake on a sheet of greaseproof paper, to avoid making a sticky mess on the worktop, and brush the hot jam all over the surface of the cake with a pastry brush. Make sure you cover the cake completely, so that your marzipan (or sugarpaste, if using) will stick well.

STEP 3 Dust the worktop with a little icing sugar and knead the marzipan until it feels soft and malleable. How long this will take depends on the amount you are using, but as a guide, if you are covering a 15cm (6in) cake, you'll need approximately 650g marzipan and at normal room temperature it should only take a minute to knead until it's ready for use.

STEP 4 Dust the worktop with more icing sugar and roll out the marzipan from the middle outwards; try to keep a round shape by turning it as you go. Make sure you sweep plenty of icing sugar under the marzipan as you go along, so that it doesn't stick to the worktop. You can dust the top of the marzipan with just a little icing sugar so that your rolling pin doesn't get stuck, but try not to use too much or it might dry out, making it more likely to rip and crack when you put it on the cake.

NEVER flip the marzipan over like you would for pastry; it will cause it to become much too dry. Just continuously turn it and make sure you have enough icing sugar underneath.

STEP 5 You need to roll the marzipan large enough to cover both the top and the sides of your cake. Once it's rolled out, to check if you have enough without having to lift it up and place it on the cake, hold a tin or board the same size as your cake over the middle of the marzipan. As long as you have at least 8cm (3in) excess around the edge of the circle, you have enough to cover the entire cake.

STEP 6 Once the marzipan is rolled and ready, roll it gently over the rolling pin. This will make it easier to lay the marzipan on the cake without tearing it. It will also allow you to take a few seconds to line it up in the centre, rather than having to stretch it over both arms to lay it on the cake. Another benefit is that you can roll the marzipan onto the cake slowly, which helps prevent air bubbles becoming trapped underneath it.

STEP 7 Now hold the rolling pin above the cake, with the centre of the pin positioned roughly in the middle of the cake. Lift the marzipan up and start to unroll it, leaving just enough hanging down on the side facing you and rolling the rest away from

you over the top of the cake. The excess should drape around the sides of the cake and go right down to cover the base board that is adhered to the bottom of your cake.

STEP 8 Work as quickly as you can to smooth the marzipan onto the cake, using your hands to smooth the top, from the centre outwards towards the edges, making sure to press out any air that may be trapped under the marzipan. To guarantee a very smooth finish, you can use a cake smoother to gently press and smooth over the top of the cake.

STEP 9 Once the top is smooth, gently press around the top edge to fold the marzipan down over the sides. Be careful not to pull it down or it may rip, and don't press so hard that you leave fingerprints. Smooth the marzipan onto the sides, taking care not to create any folds or creases; if you do get these, gently lift the marzipan back up again just where the crease is appearing and push out the fold towards the base of the base board.

STEP 10 When your cake is covered with the marzipan, use a small knife to cut away as much of the excess as you can, leaving just

a small border of marzipan lying on the worktop; around a 2.5cm or so. You can save the trimmings for another use; immediately pop them into a food bag and seal, as marzipan dries out fairly quickly. There is no need to refrigerate this.

STEP 11 For the next part, you need to lift the cake up to ensure you get a perfectly straight edge at the bottom of the marzipan, as opposed to cutting off the remaining excess directly on the worktop. Carefully lift up the cake and hold underneath the centre of the base board.

Lifting the cake can be difficult, especially if it is large and heavy. If you don't have a turntable, use a few stacked cake boards a couple of inches smaller than the cake to elevate it from the worktop so that you can work with it at eye level and move it around more easily. Otherwise, find something in your kitchen that you can use to lift up the cake — a can of beans is perfect under a 10cm (4in) cake, or use an upturned bowl or pot. Whatever you use, it needs to be at least 2.5cm or so smaller than the cake itself.

STEP 12 With the cake raised, use either the flat of your hand or, preferably, a side smoother, to gently press the marzipan onto the sides of the cake, right down to the edge of the bottom of the cake board, so that there is marzipan hanging lower than the base of the board. Press all the way around the cake until you are happy that the marzipan is smooth and even.

STEP 13 Now take a small, sharp, clean knife and, holding it at a 90-degree angle to the sides of the cake, run it all the way around the underside of the cake board. Do this carefully, trimming off all the excess marzipan and allowing it to drop onto the worktop.

STEP 14 You now have a perfectly trimmed cake, with straight sides that are coated right down to the bottom of the cake board. Place the covered cake onto a cake board at least 2.5cm (1in), or ideally 5cm (2in), larger than the cake.

STEP 15 Now you can pay more attention to the cake's surface and sides. Check for obvious air bubbles under the surface; if you notice any, gently insert your pin tool or pin into them and expel the air by gently pressing it out through the hole, then gently smooth over the hole with your fingers.

STEP 16 Bend down so the cake is at eye level, allowing you to judge the straightness of the top and sides more accurately. Smooth over the top, sides and edges as best you can, either with the flat of your hand or with side smoothers if you have them, until you are pleased with the finish. If using smoothers, you can press quite firmly to eliminate any bumps, but take care not to press too hard if using your hands, or you'll create fingerprint indentations.

STEP 17 Check once more for any air bubbles and expel using the pin tool or pin as before, then press lightly with your top smoother to ensure the surface is even. Sometimes, inevitably, you will miss these bubbles and return the next day to see a huge bulge under your icing or coating – incredibly frustrating. All you can do is pop with the pin tool and gently smooth over with a side or top smoother. You will always get the odd lump and bump and it really doesn't matter too much as you will be covering this layer with a layer of sugarpaste.

STEP 18 Once you have covered your cake with marzipan, it is best to leave this to dry until the next day so that it can 'skin over' and will hold its neat shape when you add the sugarpaste layer.

Sometimes, especially in warm weather, if there's too much buttercream inside a cake, you get a really unsightly bulge that appears in the middle of the cake and can be seen through the icing. This is known as the cake 'blowing'. If you have already covered the cake with marzipan and this happens on the following day, you can at least try to trim away some of the bulge before you ice the cake. To help prevent the cake from 'blowing', use a pin tool (or a clean pin, but be careful not to leave it lying around) and prick several holes around your cake .

SECOND COAT: SUGARPASTE

On the second day, you need to apply the next coat, this time of sugarpaste. You've already done the hard work — you've made sure your cake has a great base level, tweaked it if needed, and covered it in marzipan or an initial coat of sugarpaste, so adding this final coat should be easier.

You will need:
A cake (adhered to a base board), covered in marzipan or a first layer of sugarpaste
Brandy, vodka or cooled boiled water
Sugarpaste (see chart on page 71 for amount needed), in your choice of colour
Icing sugar

Equipment:
Palette knife, or large normal knife
Greaseproof paper
Pastry brush
Plastic icing rolling pin
Guide sticks (optional)
Top smoother (optional)
2 side smoothers (optional)
Small, sharp knife
Pin tool or pin
Turntable
Cake board, 5–8cm (2–3in) larger than the cake

STEP 1 Carefully lift up the cake from its base board using a palette knife or large normal knife, until you can get your fingers underneath and gently lift it completely off the board (it might stick a bit but be confident; it *will* lift away). Place the cake on a piece of greaseproof paper to save on mess.

STEP 2 Brush the marzipan or first sugarpaste layer all over with brandy or vodka (or, if you don't want to use alcohol, with cooled boiled water), using a pastry brush. You might intend to keep this cake for a while, or will be taking a few days to stack and decorate it, so you need to minimise any risk of bacterial growth under the iced surface.

STEP 3 The cake is now ready to receive the next layer of covering. Knead the sugarpaste until pliable, using plenty of icing sugar on the worktop beneath the icing. When ready to roll, you can also dust the top of the sugarpaste with just a little icing sugar to stop your rolling pin from sticking, but try not to use too much or the sugarpaste can become dry and may crack.

If you get too much icing sugar on the surface of a dark-coloured sugarpaste, especially black, the icing sugar will cause white blotches that spoil the iced surface and are very hard to remove. If this happens, re-knead the sugarpaste and begin again.

STEP 4 Flatten the ball of sugarpaste, and start to roll out evenly from the middle outwards, turning it regularly to prevent an uneven shape; you want a nice round piece to lay over the cake. Take care to roll out with even pressure so that your sugarpaste is a good, uniform thickness of approximately 5–6mm. You can use guide sticks if you have them.

STEP 5 In the same way as described for the first coat of marzipan or sugarpaste (see pages 72–7, steps 7–18), roll the sugarpaste over the rolling pin, line it up over the cake, smooth over, and trim off the excess, again placing the cake back onto the cake board and elevating it, to enable you to smooth down the sugarpaste and make the cake surface as smooth and straight as possible. Leave your cake to dry and skin over.

STEP 6 If your iced cake is for a single-tier design, it's possible to start decorating after just an hour or so, but take care not to make a mistake (e.g. if you pipe on a decoration and then want to remove it), as it will be more likely to damage or stain the iced surface after such a short time. Ideally, it is best to leave the sugarpaste to skin over for 24 hours. Then, if you make any mistakes, the sugarpaste won't mark too much and you will be able to repair your mistake, or caketastrophe as I like to call them. On page 229, I show you how to rescue your cake from a caketastrophe – there are always ways to repair or disguise mistakes, so don't panic!

Like anything in life, the more you practise this, the better you will get. If you are a real perfectionist, then you could practise with a polystyrene cake dummy (see stockists on page 234) before moving onto a cake. You can use and re-use the sugarpaste several times. It's a good idea to attempt a more basic or easier project on your first go, and once you have got the hang of working with marzipan and sugarpaste (you do get a feel for it after a while, like many other food mediums or craft techniques), you can then try a bigger, more elaborate or stacked cake project.

COVERING MINIATURE CAKES WITH MARZIPAN AND SUGARPASTE

If you wish to cover miniature cakes with marzipan and sugarpaste, or indeed with two coats of sugarpaste or chocolate coating, you can do this in pretty much the same way as described for covering a larger cake. They can be time-consuming but are delightful to make and always a big hit.

First you need to work out how much cake to bake. You start by making one large cake in a square tray or tin, with a shallow depth of about 5cm (2in) – definitely not 8cm (3in) depth like the larger cakes or the miniatures will be too tall. (If you're making miniature chocolate cakes, you don't need to make it in two tins as earlier; just one tin is fine here.) You then cut this large cake into lots of smaller ones. As a guide, each miniature cake should be about 5cm (2in) square or, for round ones, 5cm (2in) in diameter.

Measure the sides of your tin and calculate how many cakes of this size it will give. I always allow for some loss at the edges where the sponge may be dry, so I minus off one cake in each direction. For example, a 25cm (10in) square tin will give five across and five down, but once you minus a cake in each direction, that gives four by four, resulting in approximately 16 mini cakes. If you need more miniatures than your tin will give, bake more than one cake.

Once your cake is baked, leave to cool, then (unless it's a fruit cake) slice once horizontally and fill with buttercream or your chosen filling. You are now ready to create and cover your miniature cakes.

You will need:
A 23cm (9in) square cake, split and filled with a layer of buttercream (unless it's a fruit cake). This will make 9 mini cakes
Apricot jam
Icing sugar
1.25 kg marzipan, sugarpaste or chocolate paste
Brandy, vodka or cooled boiled water

Equipment:
Round cookie cutter (or round sugarcraft cutter, diameter 5cm/2in), or a long, sharp knife if making square cakes
5cm (2in) round or square cake cards (or pre-cut circles/squares of greaseproof paper or card)
Pastry brush
Plastic icing rolling pin
2 side smoothers
Palette knife (or small normal knife)
Pin tool
Sharp knife

STEP 1 Carefully cut out your little cakes. This is easiest if the cake is at room temperature. For round ones, press out with a cutter. For square ones, slice the cake into strips 5cm (2in) wide, then cut across these at 5cm (2in) intervals to give cubes. Pop

them all onto a large cake board and place in the fridge, as it's easier to cover them when cold and firmed up.

STEP 2 Start by covering just four small cakes at a time, until you get quicker, especially when using sugarpaste, as it dries out fast. Brush each cake all over with boiled apricot jam (see page 72) and spread them out so that you can work on each one.

STEP 3 Take some of your covering – for four cakes, 500g is enough – and roll out as described in the method for marzipan (see page 72–3, steps 3–5), to at least 30cm (12in) square.

STEP 4 Cut the covering into small squares, each one large enough to cover a little cake morsel – about 15cm (6in) square is enough. Place a square on top of each cake.

STEP 5 With your hands, roughly smooth over the top and sides until each cake is covered. They will end up a bit rough, but you will finish these off with smoothers. (Smoothers are a must for these cakes; you can't make perfectly iced mini cakes with just your fingers and hands I'm afraid.)

STEP 6 Using a sharp knife, cut off the excess covering very close to the base of each cake.

STEP 7 If your cakes are round, press your pair of smoothers against opposite sides of the cake and run the smoothers all around the edge with a backwards-and-forwards motion, until the edges are smooth and neat. Pat the top down so that it looks straight and level, and keep pushing the sides and patting the top until you have a good upright shape.

STEP 8 For square cakes, just pat the cake by pushing the smoothers on opposite sides, pressing the covering onto the cake, then switch to the other sides until you have moulded a rough square shape. Also pat down the top, to make sure it's flat and level.

STEP 9 Once you have finished smoothing, lift the cakes carefully with a palette knife or small normal knife and place on a large cake board or baking sheet lined with greaseproof paper to dry overnight.

STEP 10 The next day, line up your base cards or cut-out greaseproof pieces, and use a dab of boiled apricot jam to adhere the cakes onto the bases. Chill in the fridge for about an hour, so that they set nice and firm. This will ensure that they hold their shape and will make it easier to cover them with the next layer of sugarpaste (if the cakes are left at room temperature, the marzipan can become crumbly and be easily pressed out of shape.)

STEP 11 Cover with a second coating in the same way, but this time using brandy, vodka or cooled boiled water, instead of jam, to stick the second coat to the base coat. Leave to dry overnight before decorating. (See pages 182–9 for some design ideas for mini cakes.)

COVERING WITH ROYAL ICING

Royal icing can be used to cover a whole cake. It used to be the only way to decorate wedding cakes, until a few years ago, when sugarpaste became popular and widely available. Cakes covered with royal icing do look more old-fashioned, and the icing sets very hard, but it can give you a cool retro look. It's also great for covering Christmas cakes, as it can make them look like they're covered in snow!

Applying royal icing is quite a tricky skill to learn and many cake decorators don't do it nowadays. If you want to have a go, I would recommend investing in a straight edge tool and a side scraper. It really is worth it, and being stainless steel, they last forever.

With royal icing you really need two coats, or, even better, three, so you should aim to leave your cake overnight after the first coat before beginning the whole process again the next day. When you are new to cake decorating, you might even need a fourth coat until you are happy with the finish. Again, it depends on how you will be decorating the cake.

If you are using royal icing to cover a cake, you can add glycerine (about 1 teaspoon per 500g royal icing), which softens the icing, so that you can cut more easily through the iced surface. Without this, it sets hard like plaster, so it's really difficult to cut into.

If you are trying this for the first time, you may want to think about decorating your royal-iced cake with lots of floral decorations, etc. That way, it won't matter too much if the surface isn't completely smooth as there won't be lots of it showing. You can cheat by hiding imperfections!

You will need:
A cake, covered in marzipan (see pages 71–77)
Royal icing (see page 52); slightly thicker than
 soft peak is ideal – stiff enough to apply and
 smooth out, but not so soft that it loses shape
 (you need approx. 800g for a 20cm/8in round
 cake)

Equipment:
Cake board, 5–8cm (2–3in) larger than the cake
Turntable
Palette knife
Straight edge tool (or plastic 30cm/12in ruler)
Side scraper
Sharp knife
Pastry brush

STEP 1 Have your royal icing ready at the right consistency and cover it with a clean, damp cloth to stop it from skinning over.

STEP 2 Place your marzipan-covered cake on the cake board and position centrally onto the turntable.

STEP 3 For a round cake (I will explain how to cover a square cake in a moment), use the palette knife to place a large blob of royal icing onto the side of your cake. Spread it evenly around the edge in a generous layer with a gentle pushing motion, paddling the icing from side to side in small movements to spread it out to an even thickness. Turn the cake on your turntable as you go, until all of the sides are covered with a layer approximately 5mm thick. Paddling in this way helps to push out and displace bubbles from the icing. (If you are a perfectionist, you can paddle out the icing on the work surface first to remove bubbles. It depends on how you'll be decorating the cake as to how smooth your icing needs to be.) Don't worry about getting it really neat; just get an even amount on there, as you will smooth this over in a moment.

STEP 4 Hold the side scraper at a slight angle (about 15–20 degrees) against the side of the cake. With your other hand, take hold of the turntable at the back of the cake, just behind the scraper. Slowly, but without stopping, revolve the cake a full circle in one continuous motion.

STEP 5 When the entire surface is smooth, lift the scraper away from the side. This will leave a visible take-off mark, but the more you practise – and after further coats of icing – the less this mark will be noticeable. If you are unhappy with your first attempt,

then re-paddle the sides and have another go. When finished, clean the scraper.

If you are covering a square cake, apply the royal icing to two opposite sides and let these dry for at least 2 hours, before coming back to your cake and covering the remaining two sides. Complete these in the same way as for the round cake by paleting on a thick layer with the paddling motion, then scraping over the royal icing with the side scraper set at an angle to smooth.

STEP 6 If there are any excess peaks protruding from the finish point, use a sharp knife to drag down that side to remover the snags. Clean off any icing left on the board using a sharp knife and a clean, damp cloth. Clean the palette knife.

If you are a beginner with royal icing, leave the iced cake in a dry atmosphere to harden for a couple of hours before starting on the sides. It is possible to ice the top and sides together, but it is easier to do them one at a time, especially when you're just starting out, or things can get a bit messy.

STEP 7 Using the palette knife, place a large blob of royal icing on top of the cake. Spread it evenly over the top only, with a gentle pushing motion, paddling the icing from side to side in small movements to spread it out to an even thickness. Turn the cake on your turntable as you go, until the top of the cake is covered, keep paddling in this way to push out the bubbles from the icing, as you did on the sides.

STEP 8 At this point, don't worry too much about any icing spilling over the edges (unless it's going all over the place!) as you can carefully scrape this off. Once you are happy that there is an even coat on the top, of approximately 5mm thickness, stop and clean the palette knife.

STEP 9 Hold your straight edge tool (or ruler) at both ends, at an angle of 45 degrees to the surface of the cake. Starting at the edge furthest away from you, at the back of the cake, draw the tool forward across the cake, towards your body, in one continuous movement. Make sure not to press down too hard, just glide confidently over the icing.

STEP 10 Any icing collected on the straight edge tool can now be scraped back into the bowl. If you are not happy with your surface (it takes practice and patience) then you can just scrape it off the cake and start again. You can do this as many times as you like whilst the icing is still wet and not crusting; however, it will go crusty quickly – after about 5 minutes. As long as the first coat is level, you're doing fine. Clean the straight edge tool after each attempt to prevent dry lumps getting into the icing.

STEP 11 Once you are happy with the top, use the palette knife to remove any icing from the sides of the cake by carefully holding it vertically, running it along the sides and knocking off the excess as you go. Throw this excess away as it will have started to dry out.

STEP 12 Before adding the second or third layer of royal icing, make sure the first layer is dry. Using a sharp knife, carefully scrape off any rough edges, excess snags and peaks. Use a pastry brush to remove any loose particles of icing that could get caught up in the next coat.

STEP 13 Now repeat all the steps for the next layer of coating. This layer can be a little thinner; about the consistency of whipped cream.

COVERING WITH BUTTERCREAM

Buttercream can be used as the outer covering for a whole large cake and it tastes wonderful, great for those who don't like marzipan or sugarpaste icing. (However, a base layer of marzipan will give a smoother finish, but if you don't want to use it then it's fine to apply buttercream straight onto the sponge.) It is fairly easy to cover a cake in this way and the beauty is that you don't have to get it perfect, particularly if you will be adding some decorations. I have included a buttercream-covered design in the book (see page 213) to inspire you. And see page 89 for using buttercream to cover cupcakes.

A buttercream-covered cake looks gorgeous for a vintage tea party, placed on a glass stand and decorated simply with fresh flowers. If you want to make it look very special, you can add chocolate roses, sugar flowers of any kind, or even fun, hand-moulded sugar models, depending on the occasion. For a wedding, this is stunning in ivory with fresh flowers! If you want to make a few tiers, you can get several lovely stands to display each cake separately, or arrange them all on a multi-tiered stand.

For this technique, I would recommend investing in a straight edge tool and side scraper. Of course, you can just use a palette knife if that's all you have; you won't get a completely smooth look but a rougher, 'paletted', surface, which can also look good, particularly if you are going for more of a vintage theme.

Bear in mind, though, that a buttercream-covered cake is less stable, so on a very hot day it may start to melt, and once the oil in the butter has begun to melt, the surface of the cake will look all bitty and oily. Try to keep the room fairly cool, and it should be okay. You don't have to refrigerate this but you can, of course, if you want to prolong its shelf life.

You will need:
A round cake, covered in marzipan if you like (see page 71)
Buttercream (see page 49), in a flavour and colour of your choice, at room temperature (you need approx. 800g for a 15cm/6in round cake)

Equipment:
Cake board, 5–8cm (2–3in) larger than the cake
Turntable
Palette knife
Straight edge tool (or plastic 30cm/12in ruler)
Side scraper (optional)
Sharp knife

If chilling this cake, allow it to set before you pop it in the fridge, so that you don't smear the coating. Once set, wrap the cake up in cling film to protect it from drying out in the fridge. When you want to bring it back to room temperature, unwrap whilst it's still fridge-cold, so that the buttercream doesn't stick to the cling film.

STEP 1 Place your cake on the cake board and position centrally onto your turntable.

STEP 2 With a palette knife, put a large blob of buttercream onto the top of the cake and spread it evenly over the top surface. Use a pushing motion and wiggle the knife from side to side, paddling down with a backwards-and-forwards movement, turning the cake on the turntable as you go. (If you are not using a turntable, just spin the cake round on its board on the surface, although it's not quite as easy.) Don't worry about any buttercream spilling over the edges as you will be icing the sides straight away. You should have a coating that's not too thick, but enough to cover any lumps and bumps; around 5mm is perfect.

STEP 3 Now take some more buttercream on the knife and start to apply this onto the sides of the cake in thick blobs, roughly spreading it around the sides. Use the palette knife to spread around the sides until you have a rough all-over covering with no holes showing and the cake is covered entirely.

STEP 4 If you don't have a straight edge tool and scraper, try to neaten off the coating as best you can by smoothing all around in a sweeping motion with the palette knife, until all sides are equal and smooth. You can run the knife along the top edge to neaten any bits of buttercream that have pushed up above the top of the cake. Leave the cake to set.

STEP 5 If you do have a straight edge tool (or are using the ruler instead), hold it at both ends and position it at the back of the cake, the edge furthest away from you, at an angle of 45 degrees to the surface. Draw it across the cake towards your body in one continuous movement. Make sure not to press down too hard, just glide confidently over the buttercream. This will give you a clean finish.

STEP 6 Continue immediately to smooth the sides. Hold the side scraper against the side of the cake at a very slight angle (about 15–20 degrees). With your other hand, take hold of the board/turntable at the back of the cake, just behind the scraper. Slowly, but without stopping, revolve the cake until a full circle has been completed in one continuous motion.

STEP 7 When the entire side surface is smooth, lift the scraper away from the buttercream. If a few snagging bits of buttercream are poking up above the flat top, hold a sharp knife level with the top of the cake and run it all the way around the edge to carefully take off any excess.

STEP 8 Now leave the cake to set – you may want to pop it in the fridge for an hour or so to help it firm up. Once the buttercream has set, you can lift the cake off the cake board that you worked on (as it will have buttercream all over it) and place it on a clean board, cake stand or iced board ready to finish your gorgeous cake. Decorate in any way you fancy.

COVERING CUPCAKES
WITH BUTTERCREAM

To decorate cupcakes with buttercream, it can either be spread over the top of your cupcake with a palette knife or piped onto the surface for different designs and textures. You can use any flavour of buttercream, and remember that you can tint it with beautiful colours to make the cakes stand out.

If you want to add further decoration to your cupcakes, such as piped messages, buttercream might not be the best choice as the surface isn't flat so it's difficult to pipe neatly onto it (fondant icing is better for this; see page 53). However, a buttercream cupcake is perfect for dotting with a sugar flower, or you can top with a sugarpaste disc that you have already piped onto.

If you are making a batch of buttercream-topped cupcakes in advance, you can keep the decorated cupcakes in a cake box in the fridge until you are ready to eat them. They will last for a few days, but obviously the fresher they are the better, as the sponge will go dry over time.

SPREADING BUTTERCREAM
ONTO CUPCAKES

You will need:
12–16 cupcakes
1 batch of buttercream (see page 49)
    will cover 12–16 cupcakes

Equipment:
Palette knife

STEP 1 Dollop a fairly generous amount of buttercream onto the top of the cupcake. It depends on the size of cupcake, but for a standard-sized case (not mini or muffin-sized) you'll need a heaped tablespoon.

STEP 2 Hold the cake in your hand and, with your palette knife at an angle of 45 degrees to the cake, sweep around in a circular motion using gentle pressure, turning the cake as you go, until the top is coated.

STEP 3 Once all your cupcakes are topped with buttercream, you can finish them with sprinkles, sweets, sugar flowers or whatever takes your fancy. They look divine when topped with a sugar or chocolate rosebud and leaves.

PIPING BUTTERCREAM ONTO CUPCAKES

You can also pipe buttercream onto your cupcakes, which looks fab and is fairly simple to do. Different-shaped nozzles, such as star, leaf-tip or petal-shaped produce a range of effects.

Take a large plastic piping bag (the non-slip variety is best), snip off the end and drop in the nozzle of your choice. (In the pictures, I am using a large Wilton 1m nozzle.) Hold the bag with the top folded over your hand – this stops it getting into a slippery mess. With a spoon, fill up the bag halfway. Hold the top of the bag firmly and shake down the buttercream so it drops to the bottom, near the nozzle. Bunch up the bag above the filling and twist it until it is tightly sealed and you can feel pressure. Now you can start squeezing the buttercream out! Be sure to keep a firm grip and twist the bag tight as you use up the buttercream.

STAR NOZZLE

A simple star nozzle is relatively easy to use and gives a lovely whipped effect, similar to a whippy ice-cream. Start at the outer edge of the cake and, in one continuous spiral motion, gently squeeze out a trail of the star-shaped buttercream until you reach the centre. Lift off and up to give the top a peaked finish.

If you haven't done this before and you want to practise first without spoiling a cake, I recommend having a test run, onto a cake board, a piece of greaseproof paper or directly onto your worktop. (The first two allow you to pop any buttercream back into your bowl and re-use it.) This will give you a feel for how the buttercream comes out of the nozzle and how to work it to produce the look you need.

PETAL NOZZLE

Piping 'floral' buttercream onto cupcakes can give a lovely rose effect. It's a bit trickier than the star-nozzle method, so try it first on some paper, or just have a go with a cake – if you're not happy you can scrape the buttercream back into the bowl and re-use it.

STEP 1 Hold your petal-shaped nozzle against the top of your cupcake in the centre with the fat side touching the sponge and the tapered petal edge at the top.

STEP 2 Squeeze a small, cone-shaped 'centre petal' onto the cake and stop. Twist the cupcake round as the icing comes out, rather than trying to move the nozzle; it is much easier to turn the cake than to turn the piping bag.

STEP 3 Now squeeze out another petal to 'cup' around the centre one, beginning a layered rose-petal effect.

STEP 4 Repeat by piping a third petal around the two centre ones, then continue this by going around in a circle, building up petals, squeezing each one out and then stopping once it is formed, until the entire surface is covered with a pretty, buttery, sugary rose.

LEAF NOZZLE

Piping buttercream 'leaves' around a flower or centre decoration is straightforward with a leaf nozzle – it's all about the squeezing technique and knowing when to stop and drag away. (See pictures, opposite.)

STEP 1 Place the tip of the leaf nozzle onto the cake against where you want the leaves to 'grow' out from.

STEP 2 You want the leaf to be fatter and wider at the start, then tapering off to a point as you finish. Squeeze the buttercream out to begin the leaf, then, still squeezing, pull away from the base and gently release the pressure until you stop. Drag the tip of the nozzle up and away from the cake.

STEP 3 If you want the leaves to look ruffled, you can move the nozzle slightly up and down while you squeeze out the buttercream; have a practice a few times onto the worktop, or onto greaseproof paper so that you can re-use the buttercream.

COVERING WITH FONDANT ICING

Covering a cake in fondant gives a slightly more messy look and does take some skill, but it's great for certain designs. If you wish to decorate a whole cake with fondant icing, you can pour the entire bowl of icing over the cake on a wire rack in the same way as described for the glossy chocolate ganache (see page 99).

COVERING CUPCAKES WITH FONDANT ICING

Fondant-covered cupcakes are often better than buttercream cupcakes if you want a suitable surface on which to decorate. For example, you can easily pipe the recipient's name, or age for a birthday, onto fondant, whereas buttercream surfaces are not flat so it's difficult to pipe onto them neatly.

Secondly, if your cakes are totally covered in fondant, this will preserve the sponge inside for much longer. Fondant-covered cupcakes can last for up to five days if they are in foil cases and the icing completely encapsulates the sponge beneath. Buttercream cupcakes dry out much faster.

You will need:
12–16 cupcakes
500g pack of fondant icing sugar
A few tbsp hot water (boiled then cooled slightly)
Paste colours (optional)

Equipment:
Wire rack
Greaseproof paper
Pin tool
Palette knife or metal spoon

POURING

Make the fondant as described on page 53 or follow the instructions on the packet. They vary a bit, but ideally you want a consistency that is runny enough to pour but not so runny that it doesn't set well – you are looking for the consistency of treacle, so that it will slide off your spoon onto the cake. If you prefer, you can fill a plastic disposable piping bag with the entire amount of fondant and snip a small hole in it, to give you a bit more control. However, a spoon works perfectly well. You'll need a generous tablespoon of fondant for a standard-sized cupcake.

STEP 1 If you wish to colour the fondant, tint with the colour of your choice. Cover the bowl with a clean, damp tea towel to keep it from drying out.

STEP 2 Scoop up a tablespoonful of fondant, slowly so that it doesn't spill over. Drip the fondant onto the top of a cupcake.

TIP

Ideally, if you are planning to cover cupcakes with fondant, it is important to bake them with the right amount of batter in the case, so that the sponge rises to just under the top of the case. This makes it so much easier to cover the cakes with fondant. I find that filling the case to just under halfway usually works out about right. If the baked sponge pokes up or rises above the top of the case, you can, of course, trim it flat, but it's easier if you start with a sponge that's just under the top edge. This enables you to pour in the fondant and for it to be contained within the cake case rather than trickling over the edge, which looks messy. Your fondant will then sit nice and flat, making it much easier to pipe onto, or add pictures or cut-out shapes to.

STEP 3 The fondant will slowly start to spread towards the edges of the case. At this stage you should be able to tell if you need to add a little more. Work quickly, as it sets fast and begins to skin over when exposed to the air. If you have added too much icing, you can invert the cupcake over the bowl (be careful not to drop crumbs into the bowl of icing) and then turn it back over once some of the fondant has dripped off.

STEP 4 To encourage the fondant to settle flat on the cake, to give you a neat surface for decorating (piping a message onto a lumpy surface will make even the tidiest of writing look messy!), gently tap the base of the cupcake on the worktop, giving it little knocks until the icing has flooded to the edges of the case.

STEP 5 Check the finish and if you notice any tiny bubbles appearing in the icing, pop them quickly with your pin tool, then tap the cake again to flatten. Leave to set for 24 hours until the icing is hard. You can then pipe onto the fondant (such as a message, name or number) or embellish with flowers, push-mould decorations, etc.

DIPPING

Another way to apply fondant to cupcakes, particularly if you prefer to bake your cupcakes with a domed sponge top, is to hold the cupcake by its case and invert it over the bowl of fondant, immersing the top just far enough into the icing to coat the sponge, and taking care not to let it smudge onto the case. Again, the fondant will set touch-dry after a few hours, but it's better to leave the cakes until the next day, to totally dry out, before decorating them.

If your fondant has a thin consistency, it's best to let a thin coating dry for a couple of hours, before going back and dipping the cakes again to ensure a good coverage without any sponge showing through.

To take it slowly but still get a perfect result, lay a damp tea towel over your bowl of fondant so that it doesn't form a skin and leave you with flakes in your smooth topping.

COVERING WITH GLOSSY CHOCOLATE GANACHE FOR POURING

The glossy chocolate ganache covering on page 54 can be used on both larger cakes and cupcakes. It is relatively simple to do and quite fun too!

If you want a simple cake project that tastes amazing, there's nothing better than a cake iced in chocolate ganache and then decorated with a corsage of chocolate roses. You can buy these in a plethora of colours at good suppliers, or alternatively you can make your own (see page 150), or you can pipe a simple message directly onto the cake for a personal touch. I have included a single-tier chocolate ganache cake in the book to spark your imagination (see page 190). Chocolate ganache is also a perfect marriage with Zesty Orange Cupcakes (see page 43), especially at Christmas!

Although ganache is a quick way to decorate, if you want to try different designs other than simple piping or adding chocolate, fresh or sugar decorations, you will probably find it's best to stick with sugarpaste or chocolate paste. It's also a bit tricky to stack ganache-covered cakes; it can be done, of course, but you need to think about the shelf life and the room temperature, as ganache isn't as stable as sugarpaste.

When you are working with chocolate ganache, ideally you need a stable room temperature. At Fancy Nancy, we are lucky enough to have an air-conditioned room to work in during the warmer months. Most people won't have that luxury at home, so if it's a steaming summer day, you will probably get into a melty, sticky mess. It might be best, therefore, to work in the evenings or to stick with sugarpaste or chocolate paste! Also, be warned that if you keep a ganache-covered cake for a few days and the temperature keeps changing, you might see matt white patches appearing on the surface.

You will need:
A round cake, split and filled, and covered in buttercream if you wish (see page 86) and adhered to a base board
Glossy chocolate ganache for pouring (see page 54, recipe will cover a 15cm/6in round cake)

Equipment:
Wire rack
Greaseproof paper or baking parchment
Measuring jug with lip (optional)
Palette knife or metal spoon
Small, sharp knife
Piping bag and No. 3 nozzle (optional)

STEP 1 Place your cake onto a clean wire rack set over a large piece of greaseproof paper or baking parchment – to catch the excess ganache that pours down the sides of the cake.

STEP 2 Now, with your ganache in a measuring jug with a lip for ease (or you can pour from the bowl), pour it liberally over the cake so that you have a big shiny puddle of chocolate on the top of your cake.

STEP 3 Use a palette knife or the back of a spoon to encourage the chocolate to spread slowly to the edges and down the sides of the cake. If some sponge is still showing through, add another big glug over the top (use extra so that you get good coverage, and anything left on the paper below can be re-used) and use the palette knife or spoon to spread it all over the top and sides.

STEP 4 Once the cake is covered and there is no sponge showing, gently tap the rack on the worktop to carefully level the topping and get a smoother finish.

STEP 5 Leave to set at room temperature. The chocolate ganache will firm up into a soft, creamy chocolate shell.

STEP 6 When you are ready to place your cake onto a board, or cake stand, use a palette knife to lift up the cake from one side, just enough to get your hands under it (you will get chocolatey hands!).

STEP 7 Hold the cake up to eye level carefully on one hand (with whichever hand feels the most comfortable). You might find this a bit tricky, but try to position your hand in the centre underneath the cake board, and splay out your fingers to help balance it. You will see a rough edge of chocolate along the bottom of the cake where it was against the wire rack. Take a small sharp knife, and at a 180-degree angle to the sides, flush with the flat base, run the knife away from you to trim off that chocolate and neaten up your edge.

STEP 8 Place a dab of ganache or royal icing in the middle of your board or cake stand; this will keep the cake stuck down. Position the cake on the board or stand. You can leave the cake like this, or if you want it to look really professional and special, you can pipe a trail of ganache around the bottom (see page 136), to finish off the look and hide any uneven bits.

COVERING CUPCAKES
WITH GANACHE

Cupcakes lend themselves perfectly to being covered with ganache in the same way as fondant, by baking the sponge just under the level of the case (fill only halfway with batter) so that you don't have to trim them flat. Then flood with glossy chocolate heaven. Make the ganache as described on page 54; it will cover 12–16 cupcakes.

STEP 1 While it's still warm, pour just a dash of the ganache onto the top of each cupcake. Don't overfill – you can always add more, but you don't want it to spill over the edges of the cupcake case. I find it helpful to pour the ganache from a jug with a lip, so that it's easier to control.

STEP 2 Once the ganache is poured on, take each cupcake in its case and gently tap on a surface to encourage the chocolate to spread to the edges and sit flat. Don't worry if your sponge is a bit domed; once you decorate it with sprinkles, gold leaf or a white-chocolate rose it will look beautiful.

STEP 3 Continue until your batch is covered, then leave to set.

COVERING WITH CHOCOLATE PASTE

Chocolate paste (also known as roll-out chocolate, modelling chocolate or chocolate plastique) is great if you want a chocolate-coated cake but need it to last longer than is possible with ganache, or if you wish to decorate, paint or embellish with appliqué for a special occasion. It is a delicious chocolate coating, made using a large quantity of Belgian chocolate, so it tastes fabulous and fudgy. It's different from pure chocolate – it still tastes gorgeous, but has a slightly chewy texture. The addition of glucose and cocoa makes it rollable or mouldable, so that you can use the paste for all manner of things, including covering cakes, and making flowers and models. It's much more stable than ganache, sets harder and skins over. As a covering, it's quite strong and has a lovely smooth, flat surface, similar to sugarpaste or marzipan.

Chocolate paste is brilliant for cake decorating and strikes a happy medium for those who don't really like marzipan and sugarpaste and prefer a chocolatey cake but still want to be able to decorate it. You can make it yourself (see page 55) or you can also now purchase really good-quality ready-made chocolate paste (see stockists on page 234). It can either be used as a flat covering, like sugarpaste, or it can be used to cover your sponge fairly roughly, meaning you don't have to be as precise as when you are covering a cake with marzipan

and sugarpaste. Chocolate paste allows you to create so many fabulous designs and is an easy and, more importantly, forgiving product to work with in the kitchen. At Fancy Nancy we make frilly fans, panels, floral decorations and figures with this. You can also use it to create crazy, wacky designs with crumpled chocolate adornments.

The white-chocolate version (see page 56) can be coloured with paste colourings, to make bright, multi-coloured chocolate creations; they look like gorgeous, shiny, fondant decorations, but taste much more chocolatey and less sugary sweet.

Working with this chocolate is fairly similar to working with sugarpaste and marzipan by way of the application. However, bear in mind that if it gets hot you may find it goes oily. Working in a stable room temperature is best, ideally between 16–23°C. The other advantage to this medium is that it doesn't dry out quickly like sugarpaste; it's a bit more forgiving.

For a 15cm (6in) round cake, you'll need approximately 650g chocolate paste. For quantities needed to cover different-sized cakes with chocolate paste, refer to the marzipan quantities chart on page 71. If you don't intend to add further decorations over the cake's surface, you may wish to cover your cake twice with this chocolate coating to achieve a smoother finish.

You will need:

A cake, split and filled, and stuck to a base board
Apricot jam
Icing sugar
Chocolate paste (for amount, see introduction)

Equipment:

Greaseproof paper
Pastry brush
Plastic icing rolling pin
Guide sticks or marzipan spacers (optional)
Top smoother
2 side smoothers
Small, sharp knife
Turntable
Pin tool or pin
Cake board, 5–8cm (2–3in) larger than the cake
Vodka, brandy or cooled boiled water

STEP 1 First, you need to make the surface of the cake sticky so that the chocolate will adhere to it. The best thing to use is apricot jam. Microwave the jam for a couple of minutes until boiling, just to be sure that no bacteria becomes trapped between the cake and the chocolate. If you don't have a microwave, bring the jam to the boil in a pan on the hob.

STEP 2 Place the cake on a sheet of greaseproof paper to avoid making a sticky mess on the worktop, and brush the jam all over the surface of the cake with a pastry brush. Make sure you cover it completely so that the chocolate will stick well.

STEP 3 Dust the worktop with a little icing sugar and knead the chocolate paste until it feels soft and malleable; how long this takes depends on the amount you are using.

STEP 4 Begin to roll out the chocolate, from the middle outwards, and turning it

regularly to keep the shape round. Make sure to sweep plenty of icing sugar under the chocolate so that it doesn't stick to the worktop. Also dust the top of the chocolate with just a little icing sugar so that your rolling pin doesn't stick, but don't use too much or the chocolate might dry out, making it more likely to rip or crack when you put it onto the cake.

NEVER flip the chocolate over as you would for pastry; it will become much too dry. Just make sure to turn it and ensure there's enough icing sugar underneath; this way you will be sure to keep a smooth, gleaming coating.

STEP 5 You need to keep the same even thickness over the whole piece of chocolate, without any bumps, and don't let it get too thin in places, or it may rip. Again, I really recommend investing in a pair of guide sticks or marzipan spacers, which enable you to roll the entire piece of chocolate to the thickness of the sticks, giving you a smooth, even surface. But, of course, they're not essential, so if you don't have them, just take care to apply gentle, even pressure over the chocolate as you roll.

STEP 6 Continue rolling in this manner, turning a quarter-turn every so often to ensure a nice, even shape. Roll out to a size large enough to cover the top and all around the sides of the cake. To ensure it's going to cover the entire cake, you'll need the piece to be as large as the cake's diameter, plus an extra 15–18cm (6–7in) approximately.

STEP 7 Once it's ready, roll the chocolate gently over the rolling pin. Hold the pin above the cake with the centre of the pin lining up roughly with the middle of the cake. Leave just enough chocolate hanging down on the side nearest you and then roll the rest away from you over the top of the cake. The excess should drape around the sides of the cake. Work slowly and away from yourself to help prevent air becoming trapped under the coating.

STEP 8 Use the flat of your hands and fingers to smooth the top of the chocolate, from the centre out towards the edges. Make sure you press out any air that may be trapped underneath, ideally with a top smoother to ensure a flatter finish.

STEP 9 Once the top is smooth, gently press around the top edge to fold the chocolate down over the sides, being careful not to pull down and tear the coating. Press the chocolate gently onto the sides of the cake; but don't press so hard that you leave finger marks.

STEP 10 Smooth all around the sides with your hands, taking care not to cause any folds or creases in the coating. (However, if you will be applying a second coat, a couple of creases can be smoothed out later – they disappear quite well, as the layers of chocolate coating merge together more easily than marzipan and sugarpaste because they are not as dry.) If it looks like the chocolate is going to crease or bunch up quite a lot, gently lift it away from the cake just where the crease is appearing, then push the crease out towards the base of the cake.

STEP 11 With a small knife, cut away as much of the excess as possible, just leaving a small border of excess chocolate lying on the worktop – around an inch or so. You can save the cut-off excess and re-use it when needed. It will keep for a few weeks if tied up in a food bag and it freezes very well too.

STEP 12 To ensure you get a perfectly straight edge at the bottom, you now need to lift up the cake, holding it carefully underneath the centre of its base board. This allows you to smooth the chocolate down completely, right down to the bottom of the board, so that the icing ends up hanging lower than the base of the board. Gently press the chocolate down the sides of the cake, either with the flat of your hand or, preferably, a side smoother, until you are happy that it is smooth and straight enough.

Some people have difficulty lifting the cake like this, especially if it is large and heavy. You can use a turntable if you have one, or elevate the cake on a few stacked cake boards an inch or two smaller than the cake. Otherwise, find something in your kitchen that you can use instead — a can of beans is perfect under a 10cm (4in) cake, or use an upturned bowl or pot.

STEP 13 Once you have finished smoothing down the sides, run a small, sharp, clean knife all the way around the underside of the cake board, at a 90-degree angle to the sides of the cake, to carefully trim off the remaining excess chocolate onto the worktop, until you have a perfectly trimmed cake, with straight sides and coating that goes right down to its base. Place the covered cake onto a clean cake board 5–8cm (2–3 in) larger than the cake.

STEP 14 Now you can pay more attention to the cake's surface and sides. If you notice any air bubbles, use the pin tool to puncture the coating and smooth the air out through the hole.

STEP 15 Bend down until the cake is at eye level, so that you can judge the straightness of the top and sides more accurately. Smooth the top and sides as best you can, either with the flat of your hand or side smoothers if you have them, until you are pleased with the finish. If you are using smoothers, you can press quite firmly to eliminate bumps, but if you are using your hands, take care to not press too hard or you'll leave finger impressions.

STEP 16 Leave this first coating to dry overnight, then continue the next day, applying a second coat in exactly the same way, but this time using vodka, brandy or cooled boiled water to stick on the coating, rather than jam. Take extra care not to crease or fold the coating as this will be your top and final layer.

STEP 17 You now have a smooth, chocolate-coated base cake that you can decorate in a more elaborate way, adding chocolate or sugar embellishments, shapes or flowers. You can also paint onto this surface. What a great chocolatey alternative to sugarpaste!

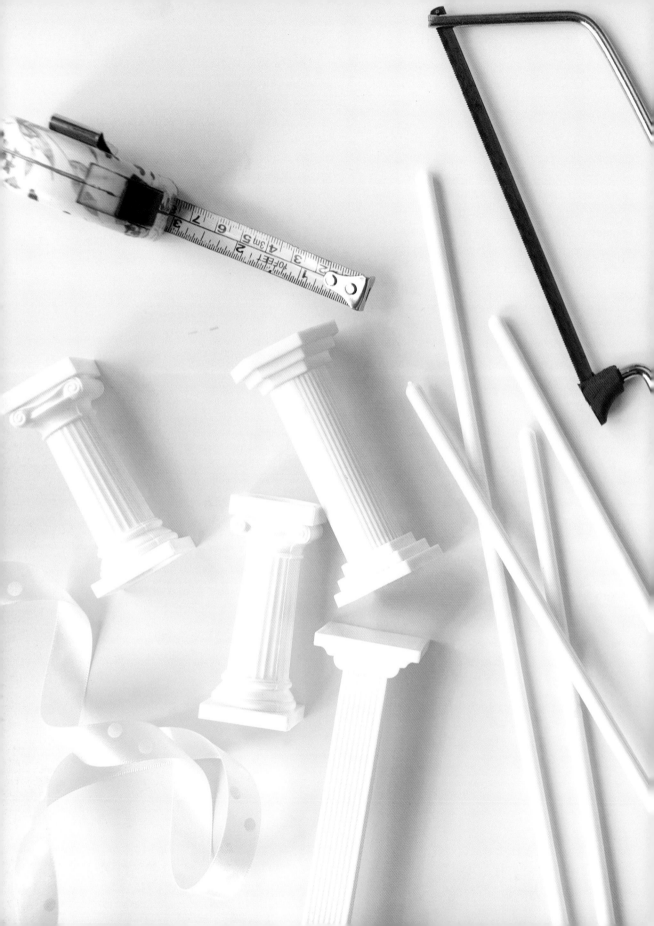

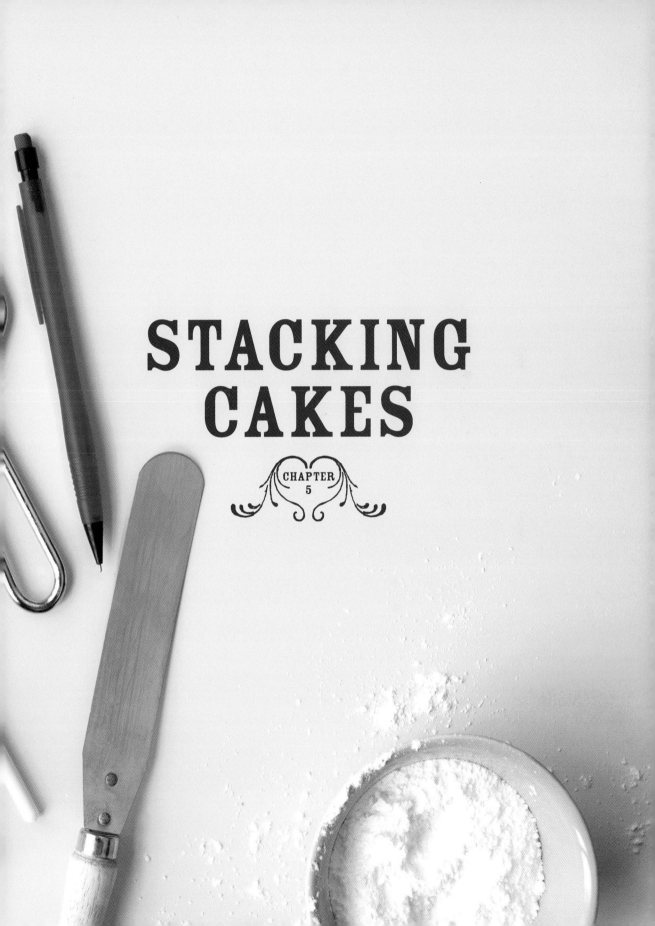

STACKING
CAKES

CHAPTER
5

There are several ways in which you can build tiered cakes. They all have their pros and cons, and it's always best to have a trial run if you are planning on making a really special cake, such as a wedding cake. The days of stacking cakes with those white plastic (and rather naff!) pillars are mostly gone. (However, some people do still use this method, and it can look quite retro, which does suit some designs, so I will include instructions for this method anyway.)

My favourite way of presenting tiered cakes is to stack tiers directly on top of each other, creating a one-piece cake design. Most of the wedding cakes you see today, as well as birthday cakes, are tiered in this way. It's relatively simple to do, as long as you follow the steps properly.

Alternatively, you might want to display your cake with separated tiers. This adds height and also allows you to incorporate other things into the design, including flowers, fabrics or sugar decorations. For this, I either use cake boards (easy to buy from anywhere) or polystyrene separators (see page 234 for stockists). When it's all fully constructed, it's much more stable than a one-piece cake, plus you can transport all the cakes separately, so you don't have to drive at 20mph and panic when you see a speed hump!

STACKED CAKES –
PROS AND CONS AND WHAT
TO BEAR IN MIND

Before you decide on a method for stacking, think about a few key questions to help make up your mind on the best approach.

Does the cake need to be stacked before decorating? For example, if your cake will have sugar decorations or flowing patterns going across it, it may be easier to stack the tiers beforehand.

Can you decorate the tiers separately and stack them at your venue? Think about the weight of a finished five-tier cake. They are very heavy when fully decorated; a five-tier cake weighs about 30kg! Imagine the difficulty of carrying a delicate cake like this all by yourself and keeping it level.

Are you able to transport your stacked cake? If so, how? If your cake is more than two tiers high, it won't fit into some models of car. Cakes must be placed in the boot on a flat base. NEVER place on a seat!

Always take a repair kit with you if you are setting up a tiered cake. If you find hairline cracks or larger cracks on the lower tiers, it means you haven't used enough dowels. CAKETASTROPHE! Never fear, if the cracks are small you can fill them with royal icing and they will magically disappear. See page 229 for dealing with caketastrophes.

Don't be afraid; as long as you know these things in advance, you can plan. Then, on the day, there won't be panic when you realise your multi-tier cake won't fit in your Fiat 500 and you need to arrange another mode of transport! If you've planned ahead, you'll have borrowed a big-enough car or persuaded a friend to drive you (or bribed them with cake!).

If you do decide to build a large pre-stacked cake, as long as you put dowels in your cake correctly and follow the steps on pages 112–115, you will be fine.

Having said all that, if at all possible it's best to make a large cake in separate sections, decorated separately, and then stack them on site. You'll need to take along some royal icing and a palette knife to lift the cakes onto each other, but as you will have already inserted the dowels at home in your kitchen, it's pretty simple to assemble on site.

If this is your first attempt at stacking, you are probably better off sticking to two tiers to get the hang of it. Of course, once you get into the swing of things, you can add more tiers.

STACKING A ONE-PIECE CAKE USING DOWELS

You can build your tiered creation to any height, but you must support the weight of your cakes inside, to prevent them from collapsing through the cake below. Cakes are quite heavy when finished, so if you just placed one cake on top of another, the weight would force down and eventually squash the cake below or create big cracks and bulges. It's easy to prevent this from happening by using cake dowels; you can buy clear, white plastic or wooden dowels. You can also buy heavy-duty dowels; I favour these myself. They are more expensive but well worth it to prevent all of your hard work from collapsing.

STEP 1 Use a cake board as a guide to mark out a circle or square the same size as the tier that will be sitting above. For example, if you are stacking an 18cm (7in) round cake on top of a 25cm (10in) round base cake, use an 18cm (7in) round cake board as a guide. Put the board onto the base cake, and mark around it with a scriber tool or the tip of a sharp knife. You can then easily see where you need to place dowels, i.e. within this outline. Do the same for all your tiers except the top one.

STEP 2 By eye, insert the cake dowels into the cake, pushing them right in until they touch the board underneath, taking care to put them in straight, not leaning at an angle. Place them all around the inside edge of the outline and then a few in the middle just to be safe. I recommend being over-cautious and adding plenty of these dowels, particularly

to the base tier if there will be more than one other tier above it. However, for a tiny top tier that doesn't weigh much, you won't need many dowels under it – for example, four regular dowels is plenty for supporting a 10cm (4in) cake – so do use your judgement.

STEP 3 Once all the dowels are inserted into your cake, you need to put a mark on each dowel (I find a pencil with a retractable lead most accurate here), level with the iced surface. Mark them all, even if your surface is pretty straight, as there will be slight undulations and you will see that when you remove the dowels and line them up together against a flat edge, the marks will vary a tad.

STEP 4 To ensure your next cake will sit level, you then need to re-mark all of the dowels at the same point as the tallest original depth mark. This way, the next cake won't be pressing anywhere on the cake below, which could cause cracks. Now cut all the dowels down to the marks – you can do this with a small hacksaw or a serrated knife but take care. Then place the cut-down dowels back into your cake, ready to receive the tier above.

My dad, George, had a clever idea for safely cutting the dowels. He got a short offcut of garden decking with lined ridges. You can lay your dowels snugly in the ridge to prevent them slipping around on the worktop while you are cutting through them. This avoids injuries and also makes life easier.

STEP 5 Once all your cakes have their dowels, you can lift up the upper tiers with a palette knife and safely position each onto the cake below. Before you add each tier, apply royal icing to the middle of the cake underneath to act as sugary cement to adhere them together, making sure they set fast and stay put.

STEP 6 If there are any gaps between your tiers caused by dowels that rise above the surface of the cake, they can be filled with royal icing, or hidden with ribbon if it's used in your design. Most cakes will have ribbon to finish the tiers; it disguises any inevitable rough edges at the bottom of your cake. You can also use pearl piping as a decorative trim around the tiers (see page 134); it, too, will disguise any gaps.

SEPARATED STACKED CAKES

Making a separated stacked cake uses a similar method to the one for regular one-piece stacked cakes but includes one large plinth or column between each tier. These add height and give your design a different look, with a colour block of ribbon, fabric, icing or even floral decoration in between the cakes.

For the columns between your tiers, you can either use cake boards, stuck together to achieve any height you want, or polystyrene cake dummies, 5–8cm (2–3in) in height (see page 234 for stockists). If you are going to put fresh or sugar flowers around your tiers, you can leave the central columns bare, as they won't show once you have added the flowers. Otherwise, you can glue pretty ribbons or fabric onto the stuck-together boards or polystyrene dummies. If using boards, you can even ice them with sugarpaste.

STEP 1 Place the board or dummy on top of the base cake as a guide, and mark around the edge with a scriber tool or sharp knife so that you can see the outline inside which you need to place dowels. Repeat with the other tiers, using the appropriate column as a guide.

STEP 2 Now continue in the same way as described for the one-piece stacked cake (see page 112, steps 2–4), placing your dowels into the cake and marking, then cutting and inserting back into your cake.

STEP 3 Once all of your cakes have their dowels inserted, it's simply a matter of stacking the cakes like building blocks. You can do this at the party or venue very easily. You don't have to stick them together, as the weight of the cakes should be enough to hold them in place, but it's not a bad idea to stick them with some royal icing as it will be safer, particularly if the cake is anywhere near a springy dance floor, etc.! It can also be helpful to stick each polystyrene or cake-board column onto the cake below in advance, so that they are all ready to go when you come to stack the cake.

CONSTRUCTING ICED SUGAR DISPLAY STANDS FOR CUPCAKES

An iced sugar cake stand is a fantastic centrepiece for displaying miniature iced cakes or cupcakes. Of course, you can use ready-made wedding and cupcake stands, but this is a perfect way to tie the stand in to the rest of your look. For example, if you have made lots of floral cupcakes, you can make a stand with any type or colour of icing or covering, to display them all in a three-, four- or five-tier arrangement.

This is really simple to do. All you need is several pre-iced cake boards (see pages 23–5) in your colour of choice, or several colours, or even covered with printed images – the world's your oyster. You can use round, square, hexagonal, heart-shaped or petal-shaped boards.

I like to use boards with a 5–8cm (2–3in) difference in size between them, e.g. a four-tier stand using 15cm, 20cm, 25cm and 30cm (6in, 8in, 10in and 12in) boards, or if you want to display lots and lots of cakes, a five-tier stand with 15cm, 23cm, 30cm, 38cm and 46cm (6in, 9in, 12in, 15in and 18in) boards. You can make mini three-tiered ones too, using 20cm, 25cm and 30cm (8in, 10in and 12in) boards. Of course it depends on the number of cakes you have and the size of the party.

As well as boards, you will also need polystyrene plinths or separators to act as the central column. You can buy these from many cake-decorating shops and online sites, including eBay. Cake dummies are the best thing to use for this.

Alternatively, you can stick several cake boards together to get a height of around 8cm (3in), though this method is more expensive. Sizewise, the diameter needs to be wide enough to support the cake board above, but small enough to allow room around the column for your cakes. I've specified sizes but of course you can make a sugar stand in any size you wish.

The central columns can be wrapped in ribbon, which ties in with the design of your cakes for a perfect finish.

Below is a handy table to give you a guide to the lengths of ribbon you will need for icing different-sized cakes/drums.

Size of drum or cake	Ribbon length
15cm (6in)	50cm (20in)
20cm (8in)	65cm (25in)
25cm (10in)	80cm (31in)
30cm (12in)	98cm (39in)
36cm (14in)	118cm (47in)
40cm (16in)	130cm (51in)

FOUR-TIER STAND TO DISPLAY 30-40 CUPCAKES OR MINI CAKES

You will need:

20cm (8in), 25cm (10in), 30cm (12in) and 35cm (14in) round cake boards, pre-iced and left to dry for at least 24 hours) (see pages 23–5)

4 lengths of ribbon, 15mm (1/2in) width, for the board edges

10cm (4in), 12cm (5in) and 15cm (6in) polystyrene cake dummies, 8cm (3in) in depth (these are used to create your ribbon-covered columns to separate the iced cake boards)

Approx. 4 metres of ribbon, 25mm (1in) width, for the separators

Stiff-peak royal icing (see page s 52 and 126)

Equipment:

Glue (Pritt Stick is best as it doesn't bleed through ribbon)

Scissors

Pin or sharp knife

STEP 1 One at a time, apply glue to the edges of the cake boards and neatly attach the narrower ribbon by wrapping it all the way around, keeping it straight and flush to the worktop, until the silver edges of the boards are completely covered.

STEP 2 Glue around the edges of the first cake dummy. Wrap the wider ribbon neatly around the cake dummy overlapping it slightly as you go. Take care not to leave any white polystyrene showing through. Once you have covered the whole cake dummy, snip off the end of the ribbon and secure with a dab of glue. Continue until all three dummies are covered. Now you have your three 'ribbon columns' ready to give you height between each cake board.

STEP 3 Take the largest board: this will be the bottom of your stand. Place your largest column in the centre of the board. I like to measure the space in front, behind and at either side to be sure it is central. Once it's in the right place, mark each side with a little pinprick, or indent with the tip of a sharp knife, to save you re-measuring.

STEP 4 Remove the column and spread a dab of royal icing over the middle of the iced board inside the marks you made; this will secure the column in place.

STEP 5 Find the ribbon joins on your board and on the dummy. Line them both up – this can be the back of your stand. Press the column onto the royal icing, checking that it's within your marks and that both ribbon joins are still facing the same way. Repeat with the next two boards and columns. The smallest cake board will sit on top of the final column. Leave them all to dry overnight.

STEP 6 Assemble the stand by placing the base level on your table (or wherever you want to display your cakes). Position the ribbon joins at the back so that the stand looks perfect. Arrange your cakes for this level around the column.

STEP 7 Continue in the same way for each level, placing the next tier centrally (you can measure to double check) then loading with an array of gorgeous cakes until you finish with the top tier. You have created a fabulous centrepiece for your event!

STACKING WITH PILLARS

If you want to stack your cake using pillars, it's best to use good-quality, substantial, heavy-duty ones. This method is very similar to the previous ways of stacking cakes, and you still need your trusty old dowels. It is done in exactly the same way as the one-piece cake (see pages 112–5), but you need to be much more neat and precise about where you put the dowels, as you will be able to see the pillars between the cakes. You also need much longer cake dowels, as they will need to be cut to the top height of the pillars.

STEP 1 For each tier, consider the size of the cake above it. You want the cakes to look like they are supported on the pillars, even though it's actually the dowels that are supporting. (The pillars are purely decorative and shouldn't be used as support; they would sink down into the cake below.) If you have a 25cm (10in) base cake with an 18cm (7in) cake above it, your smaller cake should be sitting on a 23cm (9in) cake board, giving you a couple more inches to work with.

You can do this without an additional iced board underneath the upper cakes but the construction won't be as stable. However, your cakes must still have their hidden base boards sealed inside the bottom of the trimmed icing, as this is necessary to prevent the top of the pillars going through into the cake above. You can also use other bases on which to display each tier instead of iced cake boards, such as Perspex cake plates for a contemporary look, mirrors or even china plates.

STEP 2 Once you've marked out the dowel positions, equidistant apart, push the dowels into the cake, making sure they are upright and straight, not at an angle.

STEP 3 Slide the pillars over the dowels that are poking out of your cake. Mark the point of the dowel that is level and flush with the top edge of the pillar. Take care to be accurate with this, so that your pillars will sit neatly between the cakes with no gaps at the top.

It's a good idea to place a cake board on top of the pillars and check the level with a spirit level. Just so that you know everything will be right when your cake arrives at its venue!

STEP 4 Once they are all marked out, remove, adjust all the marks to match the longest/tallest measurement and cut them down (see tip on page 112). Then place the dowels back into the cake and slide the pillars onto them. Stack the cakes and check everything is level. If it isn't level, then you may have made a mistake, so you'll need to unstack the cakes, remove all the dowels and check them again – it's therefore quite important to ensure everything is level before you stack your cakes.

STEP 5 You can transport all the tiers separately, with the dowels and pillars pre-cut but kept separate, ready to insert and assemble at the venue.

DECORATING CAKES AND COOKIES

CHAPTER
6

There is an abundance of different techniques that you can use to decorate your cake, cupcakes or cookies and this chapter will show you how to do lots of them. They are used in many of the designs later in the book, and once you've mastered them, you can adapt them to try out different patterns or effects. It's all about practice. Of course, some of them are easier and quicker to execute, but if you are baking- and cake-mad like me, I am sure you will want to give them all a bash.

Like anything artistic or creative, it's a good idea to plan your idea before you get started. Have a think about the design and style you want to achieve, as there's likely to be a handy technique to help you achieve the best design and finish. There are lots of ideas in this book that you may want to recreate or you can go online and get inspiration from other photos. Even a simple sketch will help you to envisage what you are hoping to achieve. By planning like this, you will also be able to see what equipment you are going to need.

If you are asked to make a cake for someone else, perhaps get them to put together a mood board, especially if they have a theme in mind. Look at different ideas to spark your imagination, and think about how it's going to come to life: from concept to creation. For example, you might be making a cake for a favourite aunt or friend. Ask yourself, what do they like? How do they spend their spare time, how is their house decorated? What do they wear? Are they a girly, floral kind of girl or a neutral, understated queen of chic? If the cake's for a man, does he like fishing, golf, music, sport, or is he covered in tattoos? Something about the person may give you a good idea of the style of cake they would like best!

DECORATING WITH ROYAL ICING

I've been decorating cookies and cakes for around 15 years now, so I'm pretty nifty with a piping bag, but I do remember in the early days how frustrating it could be when trying out some of the trickier icing techniques – particularly using royal icing to create run-outs (see page 129) or cookie decorating (see page 158). Royal icing is perfect for decorating once you get the hang of using it. It's easy to control, holds its shape and dries hard so you can pipe patterns including lace, flowers, beads, straight lines, swirls etc.

You may also find piping patterns onto the sides of a cake tier can be tricky when you first try it, because you are at an awkward angle and fighting against gravity. It's definitely easier to pipe onto a flat surface or the top of a cake. In the beginning, I could never get the piped designs as neat as I wanted , but after a bit of practice I found ways to make the job easier and get a better finish. Hopefully my tips will ensure you find decorating with royal icing both easy and fun.

The most important thing with royal icing, whether for piping or creating run-outs, is to start with the right consistency for the job. The different consistencies are refered to as 'stiff peak', 'soft peak' and 'runny'. (See page 52 for royal icing recipe)..

Practise on the side of a cake tin or blank cake dummy first, just to get the feel of piping with royal icing. After a few tries, you will begin to feel more confident and ready to pipe directly onto your cake without the worry of potentially spoiling its icing.

STIFF PEAK

This is when the royal icing is stiff and paste-like, so that when you lift a spoon from the mixture you get a stiff 'peak', or peaks, forming. It means that whatever you pipe will hold its shape. Stiff peak is used for some types of decoration, including snail trails, beads and other piped shapes. Sometimes you may need to add a few extra drops of water so that the icing is easy to push out of your nozzle without having to squeeze so hard that it hurts your hand, but you still want the icing to hold its shape.

SOFT PEAK

You can loosen the royal icing with a few drops of water, or egg white (pasteurised) if you prefer, so that it can flow freely from your icing bag. It's not runny, so the line will still hold its shape, but if you were to pipe a pearl trim with it, the dots would begin to sink into a wavy, blobby line. To get the consistency right, add just a few drops of water at a time until the icing feels looser and easier to stir. Don't make it too runny! This is used for piping messages onto cakes, outlining shapes on cookies and piping the outlines of run-outs.

RUNNY ICING

A more liquid consistency of icing is used for 'flooding' outlines on run-outs or cookies to create coloured sections. My preference with runny icing is that the surface smooths over at about the 10-second mark. You don't want it too thick or it won't flood, but I still like it thick enough to hold its shape and so that it doesn't run too quickly from the piping bag. If you find that it doesn't settle quite flat, either shake the cookie gently or, if you are doing run-outs on a film or acetate surface, pop the film onto a cake board (tape the edges down) and gently bang this on a worktop to encourage the icing to sit neat and flat.

MAKING RUN-OUTS
WITH ROYAL ICING

A run-out is a shape or decoration made with royal icing. First, a border or outline is piped with soft-peak icing, then it is 'flooded', or filled in, with a slightly more liquid royal icing to create a coloured pattern or picture. (When decorating cookies, the same idea is applied, by piping a border onto the cookie and then filling in or 'flooding' the coloured parts. See page 158.)

The trick with creating run-outs is to start with the right consistency of icing. I used to have a few mishaps and couldn't get my run-outs as neat as I wanted them – the trouble was always that the icing was either too thick and dry, or too runny and hard to control.

Run-outs can be made by icing onto baking parchment or, even better, film or acetate sheets (see page 234 for stockists) or smooth-textured plastic document wallets, available from stationers. Once dry, they can be lifted off the sheets and used as decorations. This is ideal if you want to put run-outs onto the sides of a cake. You can also pipe the shape directly onto the flat surface of your cake or cookie. On cakes, mark out the outline of the shape onto your surface with a pin tool so that you can just see the dotted edges, then 'join the dots' by piping your outline over the dotted line. With cookies, simply use the shape of the cookie as a guide.

For small details, run-outs or even large cake toppers, it really helps to 'trace' over a picture, especially if you are not a naturally gifted artist! For the 'Robot' ganache cake (see page 190), I printed off a picture of a toy robot and traced around it onto A4 paper, then popped this into a clean plastic document wallet. This made it easy to follow the outlines and fill in the designs; it also keeps the paper nice and still.

It helps if you rub a small amount of vegetable fat or a tiny bit of sunflower oil onto the film, acetate or plastic, to help the icing release easily once it's dry. Just rub a tiny amount between your fingertips and smooth over; not too much, you don't want any lumps or splodges of oil.

STEP 1 Make up all the icing that you need for the soft-peak outlines and runny 'flooded' areas, using royal icing (see page 52) and liquid food colours or colour pastes. For the designs in the photo opposite, the colours I used were egg yellow, dark brown, pink, liquorice and tangerine, plus white.

STEP 2 Put the soft-peak outline icing in a piping bag with a No. 2 nozzle, and pipe over the edges and sections of your design (see overleaf).

STEP 3 'Flood' your sections with the runny icing in your chosen background colours, then allow to dry at room temperature for at least a few hours or overnight. There is no need to refrigerate.

STEP 4 Add any additional outlines or details (for example, I have added beady eyes) and leave to dry for at least 24 hours. If you have iced onto a document wallet (or film, acetate or parchment), once the run-outs are dry, they can be easily lifted off and used to decorate your cake or cupcakes.

STEP 5 Attach the run-outs to your cake with a small dab of white soft-peak royal icing.

CREATING MARBLED, SWIRLED OR FEATHERED DESIGNS

Marbling, sometimes called 'feathering' or 'swirling', is a great way to create a colourful effect with royal icing. It is done by using more than one colour in a base coat of icing, through which a cocktail stick or skewer is 'dragged', to give a marbled or swirly effect.

Different combinations of colours create different looks. You can use this technique to create swirls on run-outs or cookies, or even feathered patterns on animal cookies. By changing the direction and lines in which you drag your cocktail stick, you can achieve completely different patterns. If you haven't tried this before, it's helpful to have a go on a piece of greaseproof paper or your worktop first.

Remember to get the icing consistency just right: for outline icing you want a soft-peak consistency (see page 126). Prepare all your piping bags for the coloured outline icing with No. 2 nozzles. For the flooding colours, you don't have to use a nozzle unless you want to; you can just snip the end off an icing bag (although, if you don't have a nozzle, sometimes the bag slips about and after a while the hole might get a bit too big).

STEP 1 Begin by piping an outline onto your cookie or, if you are making run-outs for cakes, over your picture in a plastic document wallet (see tip on page 129) taped to a cake board.

STEP 2 You can now flood the outline straight away with just one colour; this will make the outline disappear once it's all dried. Take care not to knock it with your flooding bag or nozzle. Once you've filled in the whole cookie or section of icing, shake gently left to right on your worktop, to help smooth the icing out.

STEP 3 Add your second colour (or more colours if you are using them) into the background colour that you've already piped. Work as quickly as you can before the icing sets.

STEP 4 Drag a cocktail stick or skewer through the icing. You can play around if you want. For the one in the photo I used an S-shape motion over the surface. You can make heart shapes by dragging through the centre of a dot. This looks really effective.

STEP 5 For some designs you may wish to add a border or finish the edges with another outline. For example, if making a patterned heart-shaped cookie, you may like to ice the edge with a different-coloured snail trail of stiff-peak royal icing, or if you are making a funky floral or animal design, you may wish to go over the outline in a clashing colour to enhance the detail.

STEP 6 Now let your marbled cookies or run-outs dry, add packaging and ribbon if they are for gifts, or use for cake decorating.

STORAGE AND SHELF LIFE

Run-outs can be applied to the cake the next day or stored away in cellophane bags until you want to use them; they are fragile so it's best to store them in layers with parchment between them. Keep in a cool dry place and leave them for 24 hours before storing to make sure they're fully dry. Iced cookies will last for several weeks, as long as they are kept sealed. However, if you have baked them with a soft centre, they won't last as long, so baking until they are very crisp and dry is a good way to extend their life if necessary.

PIPING TECHNIQUES

Piping onto a cake is a great decoration technique. To start with, you might simply want to pipe a name or an inscription. Or you can texturise the whole surface of your cake with piped designs – either free-flowing or very regimented patterns. If you are good at drawing or have nice handwriting, you will find that some freehand piping designs will come easily to you. If you're not so confident, you may find it easier to follow a template or marked design. Here are some simple ways to pipe decorations onto cakes.

If you write your message in white royal icing first, it's not a big deal if you make a mistake as you can remove the icing with a sharp knife and start again without having stained the cake or board. Once the white icing message has set (after 1 hour) you can then go over it in your chosen colour. This also makes the letters stand out more, as they are lifted from the surface.

PIPED DESIGNS AND LETTERING

For this, it's easiest to work with royal icing; ideally of a soft-peak consistency (see page 126). (You can also pipe with melted chocolate, but this is a little more difficult to control.) Get the right consistency by adding a few drops of water, pasteurised egg white or lemon juice to stiff icing. Stir in until peaks are still present but, rather than being stiff and spiky, they droop down. This will allow the icing to flow easily from your piping bag and nozzle, whilst still being firm enough to stay in place on the cake. If the icing is too runny, it may sag or drip down the cake, especially if you are decorating onto the sides.

For writing a message or piping onto the cake (or cake board) in a pattern, I recommend using a No. 2 nozzle, which will give a good thickness of line – not too thick or too thin. For a larger cake, you can use a No. 3 nozzle if your lettering or font is going to be larger than 4cm (1½in) in height; for anything smaller, stick with a No. 2 nozzle.

You can write out your message exactly as you would with a pen. Make sure you have the piping bag tightly folded at the top so that when you squeeze it, the icing doesn't burst out of it. You'll need to press the bag fairly firmly. Have a go on your work surface first to check how much pressure you need to apply for the icing to flow. The gentler the pressure, the slower the flow of icing. When you finish a letter, stop applying the pressure to your bag and lift it away from the cake's surface. If you get an icing 'tail' or 'snag' you can pat this down with a damp paintbrush to neaten the finish if you wish.

Everyone has different handwriting, so if you are a messy writer, you may prefer to print out a message first and mark it out on the cake to use as a template. Place the printed message over the iced surface and prick out dots along the lines with a pin. You can then follow these dots to make a neater inscription. Or you could first pipe the message on your worktop, just in front of your cake, so that you can see where to place the letters.

PIPING PEARL BEADS

You can pipe delicate iced beads for all sorts of designs – as single details, or a trail of them lined up against each other to create the effect of a bead trim or frame. A trail of individual beads resembles a string of pearls – add pearl or metallic lustres to this and it looks amazing, like edible jewellery! Alternatively, you can create a 'snail trail', which has a different, more joined-up look. See instructions overleaf.

To pipe an icing pearl, use stiff-peak royal icing (see page 126) in a piping bag with a No. 3 nozzle. Pipe directly onto the surface of your cake or board, facing straight on. Take your time, squeezing the bag until the pearl is the desired size (I like them approximately 5mm in diameter); when you are happy with the size, stop pressing and pull the nozzle away from the pearl.

When you pull away, you might get a tiny 'tail' or 'snag' (we like to call them nipples in the trade!). If you do have some tails, don't worry; just have a small paintbrush and some cooled boiled water to hand. After every few pearls, dampen your brush and lightly touch and press on the peaked bit. It will then sit flush with the pearl and won't stick to your brush. However, although this does looks better, most people won't notice these little points, unless they are beady-eyed cake enthusiasts!

PIPING 'SNAIL TRAILS', SHAPED TRAILS OR PEARL-BEAD TRIMS

Royal icing is perfect for piping trims around the base of each cake tier, around their top edges, or around sugar details, to enhance the design, and also to hide any joins. These trims can be made using different piping nozzles, including round, star or shell-shaped nozzles, to create particular finishes.

To create a classic rounded 'snail trail', use stiff-peak royal icing in a piping bag with a No. 3 nozzle. Begin at the back of your cake or at a convenient starting point if you are framing an image or sugar detail.

Begin by piping a pearl (see opposite) with gentle pressure. Once your first pearl is extruded, release the pressure on the bag and draw the piping nozzle away from the pearl to one side. This will create a little tail of icing on the surface of your cake or iced board. Now pipe another pearl just slightly overlapping that tail, next to the first pearl, to begin the trail. Pipe like this in a continous line or trail all around your cake or design until you have a gorgeous sugar pearl-bead trim or frame. This is a classic 'snail trail'.

If you prefer a more structured bead trim (almost like a string of pearls) You can pipe each pearl onto the cake seperately, patting down any peak to round the top of the pearl and continue by piping each pearl next to the previous one, almost touching its neighbour. These pearls look gorgeous if painted with a pearl lustre once dry.

PRESSURE PIPING

This is a bit trickier than the above techniques, so I recommend trying those first so that you get a feel for the icing. Don't try a design like this until you have mastered doing a snail trail, piped pearls and a lace/patterned design. It will end in tears!

Pressure-piped patterns have heavier, more pronounced parts through the design, and this is all done by hand. You start at one point of the design and push out a thicker/larger part of the icing. Then as you drag away, you tail off the pressure, leaving a thinner trail as you go. It has quite a regal and old-fashioned look. It's a bit dated right now, but these things come back into fashion. You may like to try it for a particular cake or idea, and it looks good on monogrammed cookies.

A simple pressure-piping technique is to create little piped hearts on a cake (see the photograph, below, or for cake jazzling, see page 199). They are lovely 'fillers' to pipe over a cake's surface. These are very simple to do and a good introduction to the art of pressure piping. Use a No. 3 nozzle with stiff-peak royal icing in your piping bag and apply pressure to eject a bead, then release the pressure whilst dragging away. This creates a pearl with a tail trailing off from it. Continue by piping another bead next to this first shape and again dragging away, completing the heart.

If you want to try a very structured pressure-piped design, it is best to mark out the pattern onto the sides of your cake rather than do it freehand. Make sure you measure the edges, then space the different patterns equally around your cake.

PIPING PATTERNS TO TEXTURISE ICING

Royal icing can be used to pipe lace patterns and texturised designs onto the icing on your cakes. It looks beautiful when finished and it is fairly simple to do. You'll need soft-peak royal icing and either a No. 2 or 3 nozzle for most of the patterns below.

LACE OR PATTERN PIPING

Alternatively, you may like to pipe a pattern (from an invite, a dress design or favourite picture, for example) and you can do this freehand directly onto the cake. If you are nervous, trace out the main parts onto paper, then lay this over the cake and prick out the design onto your cake with a pin. Then you can pipe the icing to 'join the dots' on your cake.

BRUSH EMBROIDERY

If you want to enhance your lace piping, you can try a technique called brush embroidery. It involves piping out a shape – floral lace works really well – then using a small, damp artist's brush to gently press onto the outer edges and draw inwards. This creates an embroidered effect, with the pattern slightly raised at the outer edges. It can hide a multitude of sins on the cake's surface, plus if your piping is a bit wobbly, once you have brushed it down you won't be able to notice any shaky edges.

FILIGREE

Simple filigree really is just squiggly lines. If you are good at drawing, you can do it freehand and when it's all finished and together, you can't see any particular parts of the pattern, so you don't need to be precise. It's a good technique to use if you are fairly confident with piping freehand. If not, then stick to decorating with a pattern which you can mark onto your iced surface.

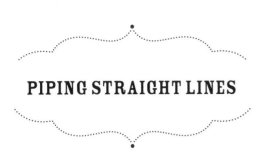

PIPING STRAIGHT LINES

Piping iced lines is a great way to add detail to your cake. You can use this technique to decorate the tiers of a large cake – or on one 'statement tier' – or to decorate mini cakes for presents or weddings. If you're feeling adventurous, try using lots of shades of icing to create an ombre effect around your cake – funky! It can be tricky at first and it helps if you have a steady hand – don't try this with a hangover…it won't turn out well!

You will need
Your cake (or cakes), covered in sugarpaste
Greaseproof paper
Turntable (optional)
Stiff-peak royal icing in a piping bag with a
    No 3 nozzle (use one bag per shade if you are
    trying multi-colour or ombre-effect piping)
Small, clean paintbrush
Cooled boiled water

STEP 1 Choose your starting point on your cake. Gently squeeze the icing bag against the cake with a light pressure, so that the icing begins to flow out and attach itself to the cake. Now lift the nozzle away from the surface and continue piping in a straight line just above the cake; don't drag the icing along the cake's surface as the line will come out wobbly. If you are piping straight lines down the sides of a cake, lift the nozzle away from the cake slightly so that gravity pulls the icing down. This will keep the icing lines nice and straight.

STEP 2 Once you reach the end point on your design, very gently push the nozzle back towards the cake until it touches the surface, then stop squeezing and pull away. If you see a little tail or snag poking up from the piping just pat it down with a paintbrush that has been dampened with cooled boiled water.

STEP 3 Continue all the way around your cake edge or across the top of your cake or cake board to create your design.

To get to grips with this trickier technique, try it out first on the edge of a blank cake dummy, upturned mug or upturned cake tin — especially if it's your first attempt.

USING CUTTERS

This really simple technique uses shaped cutters to create sugar embellishments made from chocolate paste, sugarpaste and even petal paste (for finer, thinner details). Use different mediums to achieve your desired effect.

There are all kinds of cutters available: letters, patterns, animals, flowers and many other shapes. They range from simple metal cutters in all sizes, to plunger-style cutters that not only cut out the shape, but eject it too. This is good because tiny sugarpaste shapes can be tricky and sticky to handle. There are even plunger cutters that also make an impression on the cut-out shape.

For basic cut-outs, including polka dots, hearts, stars, etc., simply roll out your chosen paste very thinly (about as thin as a sheet of dried lasagne – no more than 1mm thick). For basic shapes that will be adhered to the top or side of the cake, you don't need to use petal paste; sugarpaste or chocolate paste is best for shapes that will be attached completely flat.

You can use this technique to create all kinds of looks, from polka-dot cakes to appliqué designs. You can even go on to embellish a cut-out: try adding royal icing to the edges of the shape to add outline or extra detail, use brush embroidery on the wings of a sugar butterfly cut-out, or why not paint glitter onto sugar stars to make them sparkle? Try a few things out on the worktop or piece of greaseproof paper first.

You will need:
Small amount of sugarpaste or chocolate paste (approx. 50g)
Icing sugar
Runny royal icing, vodka or cooled boiled water

Equipment:
Plastic icing rolling pin
Cutter or plunger cutter in your chosen shape
Ball tool or cake dowel (optional)
Small paintbrush

STEP 1 Roll out your chosen paste using plenty of icing sugar to dust the worktop.

STEP 2 Press down with your cutter, through the rolled-out paste, until the cutter edge reaches the worktop. Press firmly so that all the edges are completely cut through and you don't get any rough snags of icing around the shape.

STEP 3 If you are using a plunger cutter, release the shape by using the mechanism to pop it out onto the worktop. If you are using a basic metal or plastic cutter, push the shape out with your finger or, if the opening is very tiny, use a ball tool or the end of a cake dowel to push the shape out.

STEP 4 To attach the shape to the icing on your cake, use a paintbrush to dab a tiny bit of runny royal icing onto the spot where you want to put it. (Or, if you prefer, you can carefully brush the back of your shape with some vodka or cooled boiled water; this will make it tacky.

PETAL-PASTE 3D SHAPES

You can use cutters or plunger cutters with petal paste for creating finer details to which you wish to give a 3D effect (for example, to create fluttering butterflies or petals lifted from a cake's surface). Remember that petal paste is very stiff and elastic, so work it until it's pliable and easy to roll. You'll find it is quite stretchy – use firm pressure to roll it out as thinly as possible, until you can just see the worktop showing through if it's a light colour. It should be almost as thin as an actual petal.

You will need:
Icing sugar
Petal paste, in your choice of colour

Equipment:
Small plastic icing rolling pin
Floppy mat (or book wrapped in cling film)
Cutter or plunger cutter, in your chosen shape
Foam or gel pad
Ball tool
Former (or see tip for alternatives)

PETAL PASTE DAISIES

Daisies and other flowers are perfect for adorning cupcakes, mini cakes and larger cakes, and, of course, they look gorgeous on wedding cakes. They are quick and simple to make but look so beautiful and effective. Once the flowers have set, you can dust their centres with some lustre dusts or powdered colouring dusts, to give them a realistic look.

STEP 1 Dust the worktop with icing sugar and knead the petal paste until soft and pliable. Roll out with a small rolling pin (a smaller one is definitely easier here) using a firm pressure. Continue rolling, keeping the worktop dusted with a little icing sugar to make sure the paste doesn't stick.

STEP 2 Cover the majority of the petal paste with your floppy mat (or book in cling film), to prevent it from drying out. It goes dry very quickly and once it's crusty you can't achieve a nice finish.

STEP 3 Use a daisy-shaped cutter to punch out a flower shape. Eject the shape onto your foam pad or push out with your finger or the ball tool.

STEP 4 Now use the ball tool to create an impression of movement in the petals. By adding pressure to the petal paste you can draw the edges of the petals upwards. Take the end of the ball tool to the edge of a petal and press gently while drawing it back towards the centre of the daisy.

STEP 5 If the petals begin settling back into a flat shape, you'll need to use something to hold the shape for an hour or so, until it has set hard. A former is ideal, or see the tip over the page for alternatives. However,

because petal paste is so stiff and sets quickly you may find you don't even need to leave the flowers on a former. Small daisies will usually just hold their shape once you have pressed up the petals.

STEP 6 Repeat the steps to cut out and shape the next daisy. The petal paste dries quickly, so it is best to do one at a time, so that you shape the petals before they become too stiff.

STEP 7 Once dry, you can simply pop the flowers on top of buttercream-covered cupcakes or attach to an iced cake with a little royal icing. You can pipe colourful centres into the daisies once they are stuck onto the cake.

'Formers' are handy for setting larger shapes in place; you can buy these easily in sugarcraft stores or online. If you don't have a former, there are a few alternative things you can use. You can make your own former by using a block of sugarpaste and making an impression or well for each shape with your fingers or the end of a rolling pin. Lay some cling film over the former to prevent the shape from sticking. Another useful alternative is to use the wells in a paint palette or cover balls of old sugarpaste in cling film and lay the flowers over them to dry. Even pieces of foil will suffice if you can make little wells with them.

OTHER TYPES OF FLOWERS

There are many types of flowers you can make with cutters: two of my favourites are blossoms and hydrangeas.

Blossoms are made in exactly the same way as daisies, the only difference is that you use a plunger to eject the blossom. The centre of the plunger pushes out the middle of the floral shape, creating a more cup-like shape as opposed to a flat cut out shape. It's a very quick and easy way to create a more detailed flower and it means there's no need to use a ball tool.

Hydrangeas are slightly different; it's necessary to use a silicone mould to give them their papery, veined surface. The shape is cut with a metal cutter, then the flower is placed between the two sides of the mould and pressed firmly.

Leave these blooms to dry on formers or on crinkled pieces of foil. Once set, dust the centres if you wish.

PETAL PASTE BUTTERFLIES

To create sugar butterflies fluttering upon your cupcakes, mini cakes or larger cake designs, there are fab butterfly-shaped metal or plunger cutters available. The plunger butterfly cutters even mark out a pattern on the wings. Follow the instructions above for the petal-paste daisies, then once the paste is rolled out thinly, cut with a small butterfly cutter and eject or press out onto the foam pad.

Either set these with a former, or stack a few square cake boards to build up enough height and set the butterflies along the top edge to create a bend in the middle of them. Leave overnight to set hard, then attach to your cake with royal icing. Once dry, you can pipe little bodies down the middle of the butterflies, using a snail trail of coloured royal icing. You can also use a tiny brush to paint colours over the wings and add even more detail.

EMBOSSING

Another handy use for cutters is to emboss shapes onto your iced surface. This will give a visible outline, which you can then paint or pipe over without having to worry about freehand work. This is really handy for brush embroidery or when piping shapes onto icing. You can buy embossers especially for this purpose or indeed you can use any cutter to mark out a shape. Make sure to do this while your sugarpaste or chocolate surface is still fresh as the embosser will not press well into dry icing.

If you are attaching butterflies or any fairly heavy pieces of sugarpaste or petal paste to the side of a cake, you may find that they fall off before the royal icing sets. A handy trick to prevent this is to insert wooden cocktail sticks underneath the shapes for them to rest on. Once they have dried onto the cake, you can twist out the sticks and fill the tiny holes with a touch of royal icing.

MOULDING AND MODELLING

Making flowers and models with sugar is a gorgeous way to decorate a cake, and has become very popular. For example, you can use different techniques to make little roses, or other shapes such as buttons, teapots etc. In this section you will learn how to use different silicone moulds as well as how to mould sugarpaste by hand so as to create lots of different effects, shapes and patterns. The silicone moulds are easy to buy from cake-decorating shops and once you have bought them they last for years. They will allow you to make quick decorations, which is great if you want to cover a large area or are making a big batch of cupcakes. Hand moulding requires more skill and takes more practice but it will give you a more detailed, sculptural look.

SILICONE PUSH MOULDS

Silicone moulds have revolutionised the cake-decorating world. They have been around for a few years now, and are available in many designs, literally thousands, and in many different sizes. You can find these moulds all over eBay, and in sugarcraft shops. Even general craft shops have a great selection, as they can also be used for other mediums and crafts. In fact, HobbyCraft, one of the UK's largest craft suppliers, has now introduced a section dedicated to cake-craft and candy-making, as they are now such huge trends – they even sell candy melts and edible supplies. You can also buy 'make your own' silicone mould kits for taking a cast of anything you fancy; for example, a kid's toy or a favourite piece of jewellery.

Over the page, I've explained how to use a push mould to make sugar roses and teapots; but you can apply the same basic technique to any other shape that you wish to create.

PUSH-MOULD ROSES

This makes gorgeous sugar rose decorations that look like they are made from china, perfect for a vintage feel.

~~~~~~~~~~~~~~~~~~~~~~~~~~~~~~~~~~~~~

MAKES 12 MEDIUM-SIZED ROSES

You will need:
100g sugarpaste in your choice of colour
1 tsp gum tragacanth (optional – it will make
    your sugarpaste stiffer and slightly easier
    to release from the mould)
Icing sugar

Equipment:
Rose-shaped silicone mould
Pastry brush
Extra cake board (or chopping board)

~~~~~~~~~~~~~~~~~~~~~~~~~~~~~~~~~~~~~

STEP 1 Dust the mould with a little icing sugar and tip out any excess.

STEP 2 Dust your worktop with a little icing sugar and knead the sugarpaste until pliable. Break off a small piece. For a medium-sized rose, you need an amount the size of a hazelnut. If you'd prefer to make tiny roses, you'll need a piece the size of a large pea, or for large roses, the size of a grape. The same mould can be used for making different sizes; for smaller roses, fill just the centre part of the hole.

STEP 3 Gently push the sugarpaste into the mould. Push it in just enough to mark out the detail on the shape; don't force it in too hard or it may stick and clog up the mould.

STEP 4 Turn the mould over and flex it in a couple of directions until the sugar rose drops out onto the worktop. It should pop out easily provided the mould was dry, clean and dusted with icing sugar.

STEP 5 Repeat until you have the number of roses you need, lining them up as you go. If there is excess icing sugar left on the roses, wait until they have dried out overnight and then simply brush them over with a pastry brush to remove it.

STEP 6 Once dry, you can use these roses for many different design ideas on your cakes, cupcakes or even cookies.

HAND-MOULDED ROSES

This is one of the simplest ways to make a sugar or indeed a marzipan or chocolate rose for a cake. Whichever modelling medium you are using, the method is exactly the same, but if you choose to make these in sugarpaste, your icing will begin to skin over and dry out, making the petals trickier to attach. Marzipan dries out more slowly, and chocolate paste is the best medium for beginners because it doesn't dry out. Also be careful if it's a hot day, or if your hands are very warm, as the paste may get too soft. Have a play around with each one and see which works best for you. You can add colour pastes to all three to give different-coloured roses and you can even dip the finished flowers in glitter if you wish!

You can use this method to create small, medium or large roses; obviously you'll need more of the product for larger flowers. An approximate guide to quantities is as follows: about 40g for a large rose, 25g for a medium rose, and 10–15g for a small one.

If you are planning on making a lot of roses, keep your coloured medium wrapped up in a food bag on the worktop and get out just a small amount at a time to work on, to prevent it drying out.

(See the step-by-step photographs to accompany these instructions on page 152.)

You will need:
Icing sugar
Sugarpaste, marzipan or chocolate paste
   (see page 55 or use ready-made)
Egg yellow paste colour (optional)
Vodka or cooled boiled water (optional)

Equipment:
Plastic document wallet
Scissors
Small, sharp knife
Calyx-shaped cutter (optional)

STEP 1 Cut the document wallet so that it is open on three sides, leaving it joined by just one seam.

STEP 2 Dust a clean worktop with a little icing sugar to prevent sticking and knead your sugarpaste, marzipan or chocolate paste until pliable. Don't over-work, or it will get too soft and warm, especially if using chocolate. Dust sparingly with icing sugar if the paste is particularly warm or sticking.

STEP 3 Roll the piece into a long sausage – the fatter the sausage, the bigger the rose: approximately 1cm (½in) diameter for a tiny rose, 2cm (¾in) diameter for a medium rose, and 3cm (1¼in) or more for bigger roses. Don't make them too large or the weight of the petals will pull the rose apart.

STEP 4 Cut the sausage into discs – these will form the petals. When you cut into your sausage, the bottom of it will flatten slightly where it has pressed against the work surface – this is normal and at this stage the shapes don't need to be completely round. Try to cut the discs roughly equal in thickness; approximately 3–4mm, whatever the size of rose. You can make different-sized roses by putting different amounts of these discs together.

STEP 5 Lay the plastic document wallet open on the worktop and lightly dust the inside with icing sugar to prevent sticking. Shake out the excess, or it will show up on your finished roses or dry out the sugarpaste. Now lay the discs down with the flattened edge (the edge that was pressed on the surface) facing towards the seam. The reason for this is that the side facing the seam will be pressed flatter than the other to create the delicate petal edge. Line the discs up inside your document wallet in rows of 3, giving you 9–12 petals. Close the wallet.

If you find you are very slow, you may decide to just make five or six petals at a time to prevent them drying out, but as you get quicker, you can cut out more discs at a time, flatten them all and bring together in groups.

STEP 6 With the base of your thumb (just above your wrist), gently push down on each disc to begin flattening out.

STEP 7 You now need to thin the discs on one side to create a petal effect. Gently sweep your thumb over one edge (on the side nearest the seam, so that when you open the wallet later the delicate flattened side won't pull up as you open the wallet). Press from the bottom to the top, smoothing with gentle pressure to thin it out. Make sure to do this on one side only; leave the other half alone.

STEP 8 Repeat with all the petals, working as quickly as possible if using sugarpaste or it will dry out (chocolate will be fine).

STEP 9 Carefully peel back the top of the wallet and pick up one petal, holding it at the fat base so as not to damage the thinned-out petal edge. You'll notice that the petal will be curling to one side. Hold up the petal in front of your face with the edge curling towards you.

STEP 10 Make the centre of the rose by curling the petal back away from you and rolling horizontally into a tight cone. Still take care not to touch the thinner top edge; just press the bottom part together gently to fix. You will be left with a tightly curled 'petal' centre. This might take a few attempts, but will soon become easier.

STEP 11 Now you need to envelope the centre petal with the second one to create a bud. Lift the next petal off the plastic and hold it up to the centre petal. Have the edge curling away from the rose's centre, not pointing in towards it. Line up the seam or join of the central petal with the middle of the second petal. Sit the second petal just a fraction higher than the first one, to create an effect where the outer petals are lifting up and out, rather than the central petal sticking out furthest like a trumpet.

STEP 12 Gently press the bottom of the second petal in, pinching it to the first petal so that their bases mould together. Again take care not to press the top part or you will spoil the natural curling effect of the petals.

STEP 13 You will now have a lovely rosebud, which can be used for decorating cupcakes or for including in arrangements along with larger roses. If you want to use it at this size, cut away the excess at the base just below where the petals are joined. Leave the bud to dry overnight then use it to decorate your cakes.

STEP 14 If you want to continue, to make it into a larger rose, you can carry on overlaying further petals, spacing three outer petals equally around the central bud. Position the third petal to overlay one side of the bud (work in whichever direction suits, depending on if you are left- or right- handed), so that the join in the second petal is covered by the centre of the third petal, which again should be sitting slightly higher than the rosebud. The top of the rosebud should be about halfway down the third petal. Press the base gently to secure, leaving the third petal open and curling away from the middle bud.

STEP 15 Lay the fourth, then the fifth, over the edge of the previous petal, sitting each one slightly higher and pressing it onto the rose petals inside, until you have a five-petal rose. You want the rose to look neat and uniform, not heavy on one side, so if you feel that it could do with a sixth or even a seventh petal to balance the round form of the flower, then just add more. For larger blooms, also add more petals.

STEP 16 To finish the rose, use a sharp knife to slice off the chunky base of excess sugarpaste, chocolate or marzipan. Set your flower aside on a cake board to firm up for at least a few hours but ideally overnight.

STEP 17 You can then use the roses as they are or, if you prefer, you can add a green calyx to the bottom. To do this, colour a small amount of sugarpaste, chocolate psate or marzipan with green paste colour, roll out and cut out a calyx with the appropriate size of cutter. Adhere this to the bottom of your rose with vodka or cooled boiled water.

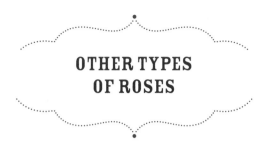

OTHER TYPES OF ROSES

There are still more ways to make roses, including using petal paste, making simple quilled-style curls or using sugarpaste to make romantic silk-style roses. I prefer the hand-moulding method on the previous page, but you may wish to have a go at others.

PETAL-PASTE ROSES

You will need:
Petal paste, in your choice of colour
Icing sugar
Vodka or cooled boiled water

Equipment:
Cocktail sticks
Five-petal rose cutter
Foam or gel pad
Ball tool
Small paintbrush
Floppy mat (or book wrapped in cling film)

(See the step-by-step photographs, overleaf)

STEP 1 You first need to make small cones out of petal paste, one for each rose; ideally do this a day in advance. By hand, roll some of the petal paste into a ball then pinch the top to mould a cone shape. The size of the cone will determine the size of your rose. The cone should be just slightly smaller in length than the size of the petals on your cutter. Poke cocktail sticks into the bottom of the cones, about halfway in, then stick them into a polystyrene cake dummy or a block of old, dry sugarpaste and set aside to dry overnight.

STEP 2 Dust the worktop with icing sugar and roll out the petal paste very thinly. Cut out the five-petal roses using your cutter and place on a foam pad.

STEP 3 Press firmly around the outer edges of each petal with the ball tool to start frilling the edges. Flip the whole shape over and repeat this process. This will give you lovely ruffled petal edges.

STEP 4 With a small paintbrush, dampen the centre of the flat rose shapes and paint halfway up each petal with vodka or cooled boiled water, to enable the petals to stick together.

STEP 5 Take a cone on its cocktail stick and skewer through the centre of a sugarpaste rose, with the cone on the wet side.

STEP 6 Bring the petals up to the cone and wrap one of the petals around the cone to create the central bud.

STEP 7 Now with the opposite petal, overlay the central one by wrapping the second petal around the middle part. Because the lower half of each petal is damp, they will stick to the base of the cone, while the upper parts will curl freely away from the cone/rose centre.

STEP 8 Continue to wrap the next three petals over the previous ones then leave to dry overnight. Repeat with the rest of the cones and rose shapes.

STEP 9 You can gently twist these buds off the cocktail sticks after they have dried, but take care as the petals will be brittle. The roses can be used to decorate all kinds of cakes. They are much harder and less palatable than a sugarpaste rose, but are more delicate to look at.

DECORATING COOKIES

Baking and decorating cookies is a really easy and simple way to get into cake decorating. They make the perfect gift and they are fantastic alongside a cake at a celebration or event as they can be tailored to suit any theme. Cookies make wonderful party 'favours' or treats to give out to guests. They also make ideal presents for children in place of those boring plastic party bags filled with rubbish toys! Cookies are also perfect for charity events or school fêtes, etc.

You can easily pick up cookie bags and packaging from the supermarket to make them look that bit more impressive. Waitrose, for example, sells an increasing amount of amazing baking and cake-decorating supplies, including a range of lovely little cookie bags.

When decorating cookies, the cookie itself must be fairly crisp, hard and unbreakable, so that when it's in its gift bag it will stay looking lovely and not break or crumble. I used to make shortbread cookies, and while those tasted a bit more delicious, they would break too easily. Now I use a basic sugar cookie recipe that's very easy, tastes great and lasts for several weeks if kept well wrapped and airtight. You'll find the recipe on page 44.

There are literally thousands of cookie cutters available and you can find a basic range in most supermarkets. If you are looking for a very specific shape – for example, if you want to make frog-shaped cookies for your granny who is obsessed with frogs – then cookie cutters like this are just a click away. You can buy almost any shape online and have it delivered to your door the next day, should you wish.

You don't even need a cookie cutter. It's really easy to just draw, trace or print out a shape, stick it onto some cardboard, then cut out the shape and use it as a template, to cut around with a knife. I often do this for last-minute ideas or if there's an unusual request for which I can't get a cutter.

Cookies can be decorated in a few different ways – you can use royal icing, sugarpaste or chocolate. The most common way to decorate cookies is with royal icing; I think this gives you the best look and allows you to create more detailed and elaborate designs.

At Fancy Nancy, not only do I make cookies to go along with many of the wedding and celebration cakes (as 'place cards' or favours), but they are also brilliant to use as cake decorations. I started doing this a few years ago when I came up with one of my most special and popular designs that I call the 'Cookie Explosion' cake (see page 217). The beauty of using cookies for this is, firstly, that anyone can do it, as they are extremely simple to make. Secondly, if your cake covering is not so perfect, it doesn't really matter, because you will be covering the icing with an abundance of cookies, so you won't be able to see if there are lumps and bumps underneath.

DECORATING COOKIES WITH ROYAL ICING

Decorating cookies with royal icing is very similar to making run-outs (see page 129). You first need to outline the edge of the shape and any sections that are to be separated off for different colours or design reasons. Your outlines can then be 'flooded', to fill in the cookie area with coloured icing.

For the outlines, you need royal icing made up to soft-peak consistency (see page 126). Prepare the icing in your chosen colour and put it into a piping bag with a No. 2 nozzle. Also prepare the flooding icing, which should be a runny consistency (see page 126), like clear honey or golden syrup – not so runny that it will spill over the outlines, but runny enough to settle flat onto the cookie. If you are making a multi-coloured design, get all the necessary colours (for outlines *and* flooding) ready in the piping bags before you start. It takes a while to make up the different colours, so it's best to get it all ready first.

Pipe all the outlines first, and any sections that you want to stay separate. Then you can begin flooding with the runny coloured icing. If different-coloured sections are right next to each other, you need to leave the first one to dry for a few hours before flooding another colour right next to it, otherwise the two colours may get mixed up and it will look messy. While waiting for the first colour to dry, place a clean, damp cloth over the piping bags to prevent the ends or nozzles drying out and clogging up.

There are also some fun techniques to learn if you wish to create more colourful and interesting designs. For example, by dropping another colour of icing onto a wet, runny section and dragging a cocktail stick through the two colours, you can create little heart shapes, swirls or a marbling effect (see page 131–2). It's really fun to do and you don't have to be precise as it's intended to be a bit of a messy pattern. Or you can simply drop in lines to create a colourful pattern on your cookie. Like everything, it's all about practice.

If you want to make quick cookies and aren't too worried about perfection (e.g. if you are making quick kids' cookies, rather than wedding favours for your best friend's wedding), you can simply use a white outline for everything then flood with the different colours. The white won't really show once you've filled in the shape.

DECORATING COOKIES WITH SUGARPASTE

This is the simplest and easiest way to decorate your cookies, but is still really effective and your cookies will look like those of a pro! This way is definitely easier technically than decorating with royal icing, so try out both methods and see what works best for you and your design idea.

Simply roll out the sugarpaste, in any colour you wish, on a worktop lightly dusted with icing sugar then cut out the icing with the same cutter as you used to make the cookie. The icing shape can then be stuck to the surface of your cookies with a little royal icing. You can even cut out the same shape from two different colours of sugarpaste, then cut both in half or into sections and mix and match to get multi-coloured shapes and details. You can add details with royal icing to finish the cookies.

I also use this method for adding edible images (see page 163). If you want to try this, simply roll out your sugarpaste and brush with a little vodka or cooled boiled water to make the surface slightly damp – not too wet, just sticky. Lay the printed edible paper over the tacky sugarpaste and the image will stick to the icing. Once the image is on your icing, you can simply cut out the shape by pressing the cutter through the sheet and sugarpaste, and pop it on top of your cookie with a little royal icing. Finally, you can add royal-icing details over the image if you like.

CHOCOLATE-COATED COOKIES

This is a very simple method of decorating cookies with not much skill involved, so is excellent for beginners or when you're short on time. Although you can't create as many designs, these cookies taste amazing. A vanilla sugar cookie is delicious with a milk-chocolate covering, or you could try different flavours of cookie and chocolate. You can then dust with glitter or lovely sprinkles to decorate.

Use a good-quality chocolate if you can – I love to use Green & Black's. Simply melt your chocolate in the microwave on medium power, stirring at 30-second intervals, or in a heatproof bowl set over a pan of simmering water. Then either drizzle the chocolate from a spoon onto the cookies, or hold the cookie upside-down, flat over the chocolate, and gently immerse in the melted chocolate to cover the whole top surface. You can leave these to set on some baking parchment paper at room temperature or pop them in the fridge if you want them to set faster.

DESIGN IDEAS

CHAPTER
7

DESIGN IDEAS
COOKIES

There are just too many ways in the world to decorate cookies! At Fancy Nancy we mostly ice our cookies with royal icing, as described on page 156. But we also cover them in sugarpaste, using cut-outs made with the same cutter that we used to cut out our dough. Or, for a truly unique cookie design, the idea here uses printed edible paper over your sugarpaste for fabulous detail.

PRINTED COOKIES

This is my favourite way to decorate cookies. It's such an easy and impressive way to make very personalised edible treats. I came up with the idea after making a gorgeous patchwork print cake a few years ago. At the time, nobody had ever made anything like it, so it caused lots of interest from all over the world! The original idea has led to many variations, including printed bags and shoes, and even printed animal cookies and camouflaged planes. I recently made a lovely printed bunting cake. Thanks to Nikki at Francis–Dee, who initially helped me with bespoke patterns, I have lots of lovely individually crafted designs to choose from. You can make your own, using photos of your own fabrics, etc., or buy ready-made. See more details below about creating or sourcing edible print for cookies or cakes.

MAKES 12 PRINTED COOKIES

You will need:

12 vanilla cookies (see page 44), in dress shapes (ideally made with cookie cutters that can also be used to cut the 'edible print' sugarpaste to match)

Icing sugar

200g sugarpaste, in white, ivory or a pale colour that won't show through the print

2 x A4 sheets of edible paper, printed with your chosen designs (see below)

50g white soft-peak royal icing, in a piping bag with the end snipped off or a No. 3 nozzle if you prefer

Vodka or cooled boiled water

Equipment:

Plastic icing rolling pin

Palette knife

Small, sharp knife (optional)

Pastry brushes

CREATING EDIBLE PRINT

If you are an avid cake-maker, you may decide to invest in an edible-ink printer. This gives you the freedom to print off photographs, images, patterns and all sorts onto edible paper. You just need a normal printer – they are relatively inexpensive – but it must be new and can only ever be used for food purposes. Sheets of edible sugar paper and edible-ink cartridges are readily available from various online sources (see page 234 for stockists).

Alternatively, if you are just trying this technique for the first time, or only occasionally need a couple of sheets, you should easily be able to find a local company that can produce printed edible paper – look online or in the Yellow Pages. There are also many national companies that offer a quick service if you email them your photos. This is a bit more expensive than producing single sheets yourself (as a guide, expect to pay around £7–10 for a single A4 sheet, so having your own printer is fairly cost-effective if you are a regular cake-maker), but obviously means you don't need to buy a new printer or edible-ink supplies if you're not going to need them again. Also, the maintenance on an edible-ink printer can be quite involved!

STEP 1 Dust the worktop with icing sugar, and roll out the sugarpaste into a rectangular shape large enough to take your A4 sheets of edible print, rolling from the centre outwards to get a uniform shape. Make sure to turn the icing as you go and periodically swoosh plenty of icing sugar underneath so that when you come to cut out your shape it doesn't stick to the worktop. (If it does stick, once you have adhered the edible paper to the icing it's likely to tear and be damaged and I'm afraid you can't fix this. The edible paper sheets do tear quite easily as they are very delicate, so use plenty of icing sugar underneath.)

STEP 2 Roll the sugarpaste as thinly as you can, ideally to a thickness of approximately 1–2mm. If using guide sticks, first roll out to their thickness; it will help you to keep the sugarpaste even. Then continue to roll thinner – as thin as you can.

STEP 3 Now you need to stick your printed sheets onto the sugarpaste. When you are first starting, it's best to do just one sheet at a time so you don't feel under pressure to rush and so that the rest do not start drying out or sticking to the surface. Take one of your printed sheets out of its packet and release it carefully from the backing paper using a palette knife or a sharp kitchen knife (if you don't have a palette knife, leave it on your worktop, dusted with a little icing sugar to prevent it sticking).

STEP 4 With a pastry brush, dampen the rolled-out sugarpaste with a little drop of vodka or cooled boiled water; don't over-wet it or your images will start to dissolve, just make sure that your brush is damp and be sure to cover all of the sugarpaste so that the printed sheet sticks to it completely, with no areas left dry or the image may lift off.

To get a uniform shape, always roll from the centre outwards. Place your pin in the middle of the sugarpaste and roll away from yourself. Then place the pin back in the centre and this time roll towards you. Don't just roll in one direction or you get an irregular-shaped bit of sugarpaste, as opposed to the rectangular A4 shape you need to accommodate the icing sheet.

STEP 5 Working in one direction (either away from you or towards you) carefully lay your printed sheet onto the sugarpaste, smoothing gently with your fingers as you go to make sure that there are no air bubbles trapped under it.

STEP 6 Now cut out your printed shapes: take the cutter(s) that you used for the cookies, and punch out the shapes by pressing the cutter down onto the printed sheet and sugarpaste – press all the way through to get a neat finish. If you are using a card template, cut slowly and carefully around the edge either with a clean craft knife or a small, sharp knife. (I do recommend investing in cutters if you can though; they are very cheap and make the job easier and neater.)

STEP 7 To stick the decoration to the cookies, use the royal icing to pipe a rough outline just inside the edge of each cookie and a little splodge in the middle.

STEP 8 Carefully lift up the sugar and edible-print shapes with a palette knife and place on top of the cookies. Press down gently with your fingers.

STEP 9 Leave to dry for 24 hours, then dust off any excess icing sugar with a clean pastry brush. Now you can display, use as a cake decoration, eat or package the cookies as required!

ICE CREAM COOKIES

Being from Leigh-on-Sea, right on the seafront, I've got a soft spot for seaside-themed cookies and cakes. I love the jauntiness of seaside stuff! I am also a bit obsessed with Rossi's, a famous ice-cream parlour on the seafront. So it didn't take me long to come up with the idea for these fabulous fun cookies. They are great for kids' parties or as summer wedding favours. To create them, follow the photographs overleaf, and play about with the colours and sprinkles to make them your own.

You will need:

12 vanilla cookies (see page 44), in ice-cream cone shapes

Caramel-coloured soft-peak royal icing (see page 52), in a piping bag with a No. 3 nozzle

Pale-pink, yellow, mint-green and white stiff-peak royal icing, in piping bags with star nozzles

Multi-coloured sprinkles and chocolate vermicelli

STEP 1 To create the waffle-effect cones, use the caramel-coloured royal icing to pipe around the edge of the lower cone section of each cookie.

STEP 2 Next, pipe parallel diagonal lines across the cones, from one side to the other, in one direction only. Then pipe parallel diagonal lines in the opposite direction to create the lattice effect of a waffle cone. It doesn't matter if it's not neat at the top; in fact, continue the cone up a little into the ice-cream section, as this will later get covered over with the swirly 'ice cream'.

STEP 3 Using one colour per cone, pipe the pink, yellow, green and white royal icing onto the top part of the cookies to form the 'ice cream'. (Or you could choose to do a three-colour ice cream to create a Neapolitan effect!) Start at the bottom, next to the cone, and pipe in a sweeping motion from one side to the other, then back again, all the way up until you have filled the space with swirled-effect horizontal lines. Finish with a peak at the top by pulling the nozzle away from the cookie while still squeezing for a moment.

STEP 4 Cover with sprinkles – multi-coloured ones on the pink and yellow ice creams and chocolate ones on the green ice cream to suggest mint choc-chip.

ROSE GARDEN COOKIES

Gorgeous little push-mould roses give a pretty look that can be used on cakes, cupcakes and cookies. They are really quick to make (see page 147–8) but look very impressive as there is so much detail on them. These cookies make lovely presents for Mother's Day, wedding favours or for a garden party. A perfectly pretty, flowery treat for all kinds of occasions.

You will need:

12 circular vanilla cookies (see page 44), covered in a circle of vintage pistachio-green sugarpaste (see page 159)

4 large, 12 medium and 21–28 small push-mould roses (see page 147–8) – sizes vary, so judge what looks best
Dark-green stiff-peak royal icing, in a piping bag with a leaf nozzle

STEP 1 Attach all the roses to the discs of sugarpaste on the cookies, by piping a tiny dab of the green royal icing to fix them in place. Leave to dry for a couple of hours. Use 6–7 roses per cookie, depending on the size and uniformity of your roses. If they vary a great deal in size, just cover as much of the surface as possible.

STEP 2 Pipe leaves against the roses, extending outwards to create the effect that they are growing from under the roses. For the cookies covered all over with roses, pipe randomly in different directions to fill the gaps in and around the sugar roses.

STEP 3 Place the cookies on plates to decorate your table, or leave to dry overnight and wrap in cookie bags.

GLITTERED COOKIES

I love to add edible glitter to cakes and cookies; what's not to like about glitter!? Add to your royal–iced cookies by gently tapping the glitter over the icing surface while it's still wet. Try making these star and cool Britannia cookies.

You will need:
12 vanilla cookies (see page 44), in a star shape
Blue soft-peak royal icing (see page 52),
   in piping bags with No. 2 nozzles
Blue runny royal icing, in piping bags with
   the ends snipped off (no nozzles needed)
Blue non-toxic glitter

Equipment:
Greaseproof paper
2 pastry brushes (1 for each colour)

STEP 1 Place the cookies on greaseproof paper, so that it will be easy to tip any excess glitter back into the glitter pots to be re-used.

STEP 2 Outline the cookies with soft-peak royal icing to create frames that you can then fill in.

STEP 3 Fill in the outlines with the same colour of runny icing.

STEP 4 Dip your pastry brush in the glitter. Hold this over the top of your wet icing and tap your fingers on the brush to lightly dust glitter all over the cookie. Repeat with the rest, then dry for a few hours.

STEP 5 Add a detailed outline by overlaying with the same soft-peak icing that you used for the first outline. Leave to dry overnight and hey presto, your twinkling stars are ready.

COOL BRITANNIA UNION JACK COOKIES

As well as being a fan of the seaside, I'm a fan of all things cool Britannia so I had a ball creating a commemorative range of cakes and cookies for the royal wedding for Harvey Nichols.

To make these glittered flags, you need to ice each section separately and let each stage dry completely before adding another colour. Start by icing the red central part and dusting with red glitter while the icing is still wet. The next day, dust off the excess glitter with a pastry brush, back into the pot, then continue by adding the blue parts of the cookie, outlining the triangular blue sections then filling with runny blue icing. The following day, fill in the white part of the flag design. (See the photographs, overleaf.)

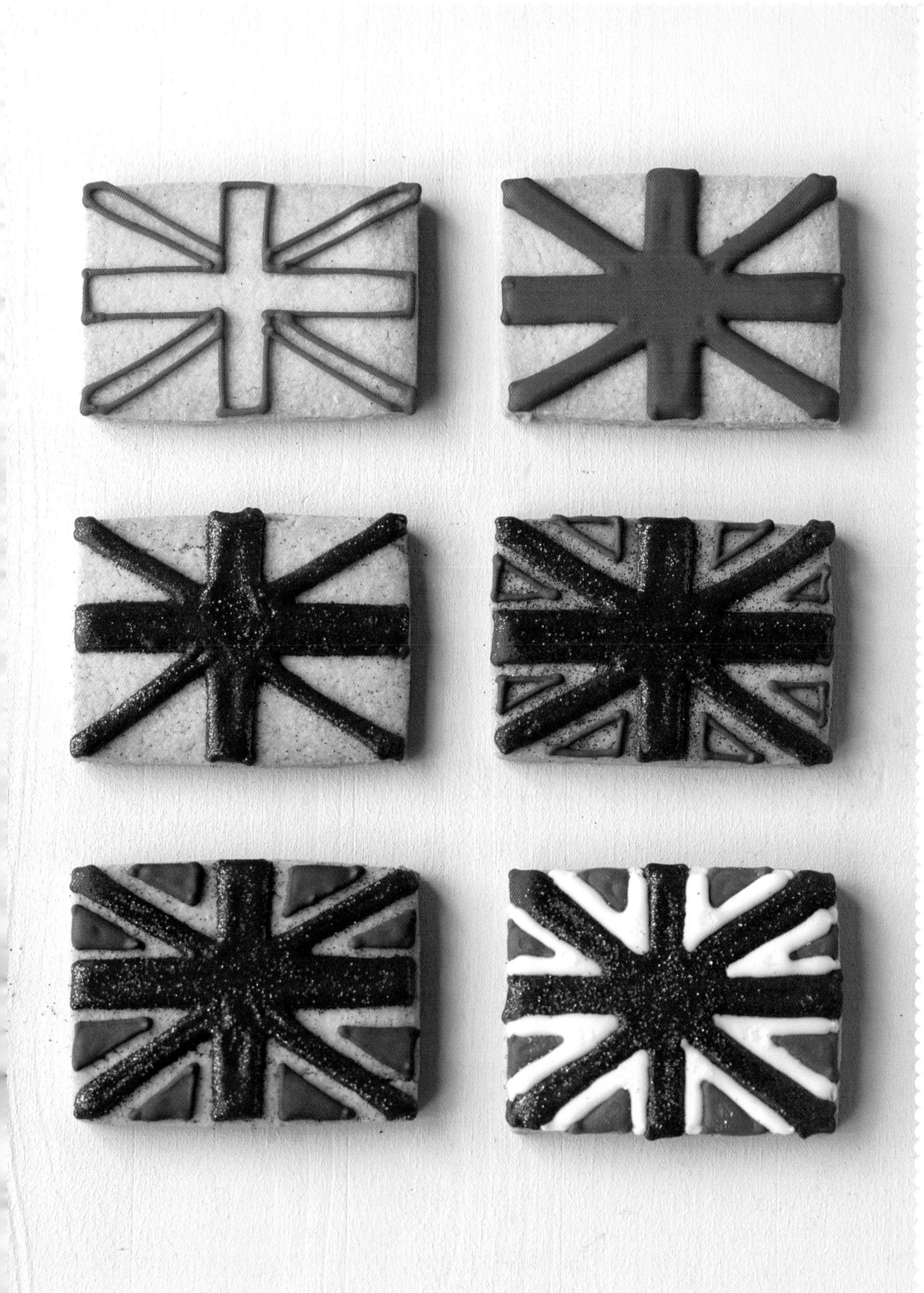

CUPCAKES

CHOCOLATE GANACHE CUPCAKES

These glossy decadent cupcakes can be finished with a glittering gold snowflake or gold dragées. Or, my favourite, they can be adorned with large, bright individual chocolate roses.

You will need:

16 cupcakes (chocolate or orange sponge is best – see pages 42 and 43), baked in gold foil cases and covered in chocolate ganache (see page 99)

Small amount of Glossy Chocolate Ganache For Pouring (left over from the ganache topping) (see page 54), in a piping bag with a No. 3 nozzle

16 large chocolate-paste roses (see pages 150-3), in bright multi-colours or chocolate shades if you prefer (alternatively, 16 sugar snowflakes cut from caramel-coloured petal paste with a plunger cutter, decorated with gold lustre dust or spray – great for Christmas!)

STEP 1 Make sure that once you have poured the chocolate ganache covering over your cupcakes, you leave them to set for a few hours, otherwise the decorations may sink into the topping.

STEP 2 When the ganache cake covering is set, pipe a small pearl of chocolate ganache onto the centre of each cupcake.

STEP 3 Attach the chocolate roses or snowflakes to finish.

STEP 4 Display on a large platter and serve as dessert at your party, or scoff them all by yourself.

VINTAGE BUTTERCREAM CUPCAKES

You can decorate these buttercream cupcakes with vintage-effect sugar roses or in a French Marie Antoinette colour-palette of duck-egg blues, mints, peaches, creams and pink. This is a nice opportunity to use gold lustre spray. Display on a duck-egg blue sugar stand with gold ribbon, or pile up glass stands on top of each other. You can buy some lovely stands from homeware shops or, even better, you can pick up good-quality vintage glass stands from charity shops for just a couple of pounds.

You will need:

16 cupcakes, covered in buttercream applied with a palette knife (see page 89)

16 hand-moulded sugar roses (see page 150), in muted vintage shades or Marie Antoinette palette with gold lustre dust or spray if you want some metallic colouring. For these cakes I have stuck to the muted pastel shades.

Pale-green buttercream (see page 49), in a piping bag with a small leaf nozzle

STEP 1 Attach the roses to the cakes by plunging them into the buttercream topping. They will stick without any royal icing.

STEP 2 Pipe three buttercream leaves (see page 95) around each rose to finish the detail.

CORSAGE FONDANT CUPCAKES

I've decorated these cupcakes with print corsages and sugar push-mould buttons. If you don't have a rose-shaped cutter, you can use different small cutters, e.g. hearts, circles or wavy cutters. The cakes look great displayed on a coloured stand, or a stand covered in edible print. You can also simply stick wrapping paper to your cake boards if you wish to make a colourful stand.

You will need:

16 cupcakes, covered in vanilla fondant (see page 96) in various colours (I've used blue, yellow and white)

16 large sugarpaste rose-cutter shapes, circles or hearts, rolled out thinly with a selection of edible print on the surface (see page 163, or use brightly coloured petal paste instead)

Small amount of royal icing, in a piping bag (for attaching the roses to the cupcakes)

16 small sugarpaste rose-cutter shapes, with a different selection of edible print (alternatively, use a contrasting brightly coloured petal paste)

16 push-mould buttons (see page 147), in a selection of colours

Soft-peak royal icing, in your choice of colour or to match buttons, in a piping bag with a No. 1.5 nozzle

STEP 1 Attach the larger rose shapes (or circles and hearts) to the fondant cupcake surface by sticking them down with royal icing.

STEP 2 Repeat the process with the smaller rose shapes, attaching them over the larger ones.

STEP 3 Pipe a small dot of royal icing in the centre of each small rose (or circle or heart) shape and stick on a sugar button.

STEP 4 Finish by piping a neat 'stitch' between the buttonholes, using the coloured soft-peak royal icing, to create a 'sewn onto' effect.

MINI CAKES

Miniature iced cakes are becoming very popular –
cute, almost bite-sized, mini treats. When perfectly iced,
they're ideal as gifts or to give as party favours.
They are equally lovely served as dessert at a wedding
or dinner party. Here are some designs to inspire you....

BASIC COVERED CAKE BALLS

These cute, round, playful mini fruit cakes make perfect table presents or equally great gifts for teachers, family or friends. I started to make these little spherical brown cakes to make the Christmas pudding cakes (see the instructions on page 185). The robins are a variation on this idea. Very cute!

You will need:

10 fruit-cake balls, covered in marzipan and brown sugarpaste

Small amounts of white, brown, yellow, red and green sugarpaste

Vodka or cooled boiled water

White, green and red stiff-peak royal icing (see page 126), in piping bags with No. 2 nozzles

Black stiff-peak royal icing, in a piping bag with a No. 1.5 nozzle

Icing sugar

Piping gel (optional)

Red non-toxic glitter (optional)

Equipment:

Small paintbrushes

Shell tool or cocktail stick (optional)

Small, sharp knife

Plastic icing rolling pin

Small flower cutter (optional)

Small holly-shaped plunger cutter (optional)

(See the step-by-step photographs, overleaf)

STEP 1 Take a small chunk of fruitcake in your hand (approx 80-90g per ball) and compact this by squeezing together and roll between your palms to achieve a ball shape (as if you were making meatballs!)

STEP 2 Place these in a fridge to firm up for 30 minutes.

STEP 3 Boil a little apricot jam and brush over the balls to make them sticky.

STEP 4 Roll out some marzipan to a thickness of no more than 5mm. Cut into pieces large enough to completely cover the cake balls. Lay a marzipan piece over the top of each balls and press around the sides. Pick up a ball and pinch underneath the base to gather up the excess marzipan. Trim this off. Roll the ball in your palms until smooth. Repeat with the rest of the balls and then leave to dry overnight.

STEP 5 When ready to cover in icing, brush the balls with a little brandy, vodka or cooled boiled water. Repeat all of step 4 using sugarpaste. If you see a little mark or crack where you have trimmed off the excess icing, make sure this is on the underside so it won't show. Leave to dry ideally overnight before commencing any decorating.

CHRISTMAS PUDS

STEP 1 Dust a worktop with icing sugar and roll out some white sugarpaste until approximately 2–3mm thick. Use a wavy flower cutter – I use a small, floral cookie cutter – to cut out five shapes for the top of the puddings.

STEP 2 To create a dripping effect, roll a small rolling pin over the shapes in random directions to flatten and splay out some of the edges into longer parts that will become the dripping topping on the puds.

STEP 3 Brush the top of each cake ball with a little vodka or cooled boiled water, then place a white dripping shape on top of each ball and smooth down. Allow to dry overnight.

STEP 4 Roll out some green sugarpaste on a worktop dusted with icing sugar to 1–2mm in thickness and use a small, holly-shaped plunger cutter to cut out 15 leaves. Place a collection of three holly leaves on top of each cake, in the middle of the white icing. Alternatively, you can pipe spiky holly leaves freehand with green royal icing. Finish off by piping three fat pearls of red royal icing onto the leaves to create juicy holly berries.

STEP 5 If you wish, once the holly is dry you can paint the leaves with gel to give them a sheen, and paint over the berries with a mixture of gel and red glitter, to add some razzle dazzle.

ROBINS

STEP 1 Roll approximately 10g of brown sugarpaste into a small ball. Cut in half and make two cone shapes. Flatten them into cute, chubby 'wings' for the sides of the robin. With the paintbrush, dampen the sides of one cake ball with vodka or cooled boiled water, roughly where you want to adhere the wings, just above halfway up. Press the wings onto the sides of the robin's body. Repeat for the rest of the robin cakes.

STEP 2 To add detail to the wings, use a shell tool to mark out some feathery lines at an angle, so that it looks like they are pointing back and down towards the tail. If you don't have a shell tool, use a cocktail stick or knife to mark a few lines.

STEP 3 With a small rolling pin, roll out a small piece of red sugarpaste on a worktop dusted with icing sugar until 1-2mm thick. Cut out little circles with a round cutter, or use a knife if you don't have one – these will be the robins' redbreasts. Using vodka or cooled boiled water, stick the red circles in between the two wings on the lower part of the body.

STEP 4 Take five tiny pea-sized pieces of yellow sugarpaste. Roll into balls, then pinch one end into a slight point to make mini cone shapes. Using vodka or cooled boiled water, stick these onto the middle of the upper part of each cake ball, to make the 'beaks'. Cut carefully into each beak with a sharp knife and wiggle the knife slightly to 'open' the beaks, so that the robins appear to be merrily chirping.

STEP 5 Pipe 'eyes' onto the robins, using a small dot of white royal icing for each eye. Pat down with a damp paintbrush to flatten slightly. Leave to dry overnight.

STEP 6 Once dry, finish off with a small dot of black royal icing in the middle of each eye. Make sure to do this the following day, to prevent the black icing from bleeding into the white.

CUT-OUT PETALS

The idea for these cool structural daisies came to me after seeing the Marc Jacobs 'Daisy' perfume. I once used them to create a gorgeous three-tier cake for a magazine photo shoot. I like the more graphic flowers; they are very sculptural looking, more like jewellery than a natural flower.

You will need:

12 mini cakes, iced in a pale *eau-de-nil* shade (I used tiny amounts of mint green and baby blue to colour white sugarpaste)

100g white petal paste

Icing sugar

Old/dry sugarpaste rolled into 12 walnut-sized balls and 24 smaller, grape-sized balls, covered in cling film

2 tbsp white stiff-peak royal icing (see page 52)

2 tbsp caramel-coloured stiff-peak royal icing (see page 52), in a piping bag with a No. 3 nozzle

Gold lustre piping gel

12 lengths of ribbon, in ivory, gold or the same *eau-de-nil* shade

Equipment:

Plastic icing rolling pin

Floppy mat (or book wrapped in cling film)

2 flower cutters, medium (5cm/2in across) and small (3cm/1¼in across)

Foam or gel pad

Ball tool

Small paintbrush

STEP 1 Roll out the petal paste thinly but not paper-thin, to a thickness of 1–2mm, using icing sugar to dust the worktop. Place your floppy mat over this rolled-out petal paste to prevent it from drying out.

STEP 2 Cut out 12 medium flower shapes and place on the foam pad. Gently press just inside the edge of each petal with the ball tool to create a curved inner edge.

STEP 3 As you complete each flower, place upside-down on one of the balls of dry sugarpaste, to help set the daisy into a large cup shape that will set hard overnight. Next cut out 24 small flower shapes and repeat steps 2 and 3 to shape and set the daisies.

STEP 4 The next day, decorate the mini cakes by attaching your flowers using a dab of white stiff-peak royal icing, either with one large flower positioned centrally, or one larger and two small structural blooms on the top of each cake, just leaning out towards the top edges so they protrude over the sides of the cakes. Leave to set for a couple of hours.

STEP 5 Pipe the caramel centres and once dried, paint with gold lustre piping gel.

SINGLE TIER CAKES

MASCULINE GANACHE CAKE

For a chocolate ganache design for a man or boy, a great way to add colour and detail is to use an iced run-out. Here I have used a retro robot to sit on top of the cake. The bright, punchy colours really stand out against the dark-chocolate background.

You will need:

20cm (8in) round Rich Belgian Chocolate Truffle Cake (see page 35), split and filled with Rich Belgian Chocolate Ganache Buttercream (see page 51) and covered in Glossy Chocolate Ganache for Pouring (see page 54)

25cm (10in) round cake board, iced in sugarpaste (see pages 23–5)

1 iced run-out (see page 129; and for robot template see page 232)

Small amount of melted white chocolate

Small amount of white stiff-peak royal icing, to attach the cake to the board (see page 52)

Glossy Chocolate Ganache for pouring (left over from covering the cake) (see page 54), in a piping bag with a No. 3 nozzle

Soft-peak royal icing, in your choice of colour, in a piping bag with a No. 2 nozzle (optional; if you want to pipe a message)

Equipment:

Pastry brush

Turntable (optional)

STEP 1 Carefully turn over your iced run-out and, using a pastry brush, paint the back with cooled melted white chocolate. This is to prevent the dark chocolate ganache from bleeding through the iced picture. Build up a few layers to be sure to seal the back of the icing. Leave to set until dry, for at least an hour.

STEP 2 Put a dab of royal icing in the centre of the iced board, to stick the cake firmly down, then lift the chocolate cake and place onto the middle of the board; do this carefully as you can't move it once positioned, or the chocolate will mark the board.

STEP 3 With the chocolate ganache, pipe a snail trail (see page 136) all around the base of the cake where it meets the coloured board, to finish it off neatly. It's best to do this on a turntable but it's not essential.

STEP 4 Put your run-out on the centre of the chocolate cake. If you wish, pipe a message onto the cake or the board using the coloured royal icing.

GANACHE ROSE CORSAGE CAKE

This girlie, chocolate-covered ganache design is perfect for an indulgent celebration for a special lady.

You will need:

15cm (6in) round Rich Belgian Chocolate Truffle Cake (see page 35), split and filled with Rich Belgian Chocolate Ganache Buttercream (see page 51) and covered in Glossy Chocolate Ganache for Pouring (see page 54)

25cm (10in) round cake board, iced in pastel-pink sugarpaste (see pages 23–5) (optional)

Small amount of white stiff-peak royal icing to attach the cake to the board (see page 52)

Glossy chocolate ganache (see page 54), in a piping bag with a No. 3 nozzle

Plunger-cutter rose leaves, made with pale gooseberry-coloured white chocolate paste (see page 56)

Selection of hand-moulded chocolate roses (see page 150), made with white chocolate paste (I use Squire's Modelling Cocoform), in muted shades of peach, pink and cream

Peachy pale-pink soft-peak royal icing, in a piping bag with a No. 2 nozzle (optional; if you want to pipe a message)

Equipment:

Turntable (optional)

STEP 1 If you are using the cake board, place a dab of royal icing onto the centre of the board to stick the cake firmly down, then lift the chocolate cake and place in the middle; do this carefully, as once positioned you can't move it, or the chocolate will mark the board.

STEP 2 With the chocolate ganache, pipe a snail trail (see page 136) all around the base of the cake where the bottom meets the coloured board, to finish it off neatly. It's best to do this on a turntable but it's not essential.

STEP 3 Attach the chocolate leaves to the cake with a little piped ganache, positioning them in the place where you want the corsage: around 5–7 leaves around the outer part of the corsage is perfect. If you want to pipe a message on the cake, make sure to leave some space to one side.

STEP 4 With more ganache, attach the chocolate roses, arranging them to form a corsage.

STEP 5 This cake looks lovely just as it is, but if you want to add a message, use the pale-pink royal icing for this. Alternatively, you could pipe a chocolate-coloured royal icing message onto the board.

CHOCOLATE CIGARILLOS

There are lots of great edible supplies easily available nowadays that enable you to create a show-stopping, professional-looking cake with minimum effort. These delicious Belgian chocolate cigarillos aren't cheating; if you've spent time baking a gorgeous sponge then added ganache icing, it's still created by you ... but with the help of some brilliant ingredients. You can even buy the roses ready-made.

This design is simple but eye-catching and would suit all manner of celebrations. Imagine it all in pure white for a wedding or anniversary. The beauty of this design is that it's very quick and you don't have to fuss over making a neatly covered cake. Aim for a cake that is 8cm (3in) in depth or make sure to measure the cigarillos that you buy. Ideally, you want them to protrude above the edge of your cake, so that you can sit the chocolate roses inside the ring of chocolatey sticks. To check you have enough roses, you can arrange them on a cake board that's the same size as your cake, to see if they fill the space.

You will need:
20cm (8in) round Rich Belgian Chocolate Truffle Cake (see page 35), split and filled with Rich Belgian Chocolate Ganache Buttercream (see page 51), and covered in white chocolate paste (see page 56)
25cm (10in) round cake board, iced in chocolate roll-out paste (see page 55), coloured to match the cigarillos
Small amount of white stiff-peak royal icing to attach your cake to the board (see page 52)
Melted white chocolate, in a plastic piping bag (no nozzle; simply snip the end off the bag)
Chocolate cigarillos, approximately 60-70
Enough hand-moulded white chocolate roses to fill the top of the cake (approximately 25-30)
Handful of chocolate leaves made with a plunger leaf cutter or a silicone leaf-impression mould
Organza ribbon to tie the cake

Equipment:
Turntable (optional)

STEP 1 Put a small dab of royal icing in the centre of the cake board, to fix the cake down, and place the chocolate cake centrally onto the board.

STEP 2 Before attaching the cigarillos, pipe a small amount of melted white chocolate onto part of the side of the cake, squiggling it on. (Only a couple of inches wide at a time, as it will set quickly.) Begin pressing the cigarillos onto the side of the cake where the chocolate is, taking care to keep them upright. Also be aware that one end of the cigarillo will have a neater edge – put this pointing up and the rougher end down against the board.

STEP 3 Continue in this way all around the cake until you arrive back at your starting point. Once the cigarillos are fixed, they set quickly.

STEP 4 Pipe some more melted white chocolate over the flat top and attach the roses and leaves inside the chocolate ring. Place some leaves folding over the edges and others nestled in amongst the chocolate flowers.

STEP 5 Finish the cake with a pretty organza bow.

For these groovy birthday cakes I've used simple, flat, cut-out petal paste shapes, made by cutting round some templates. You can find shapes online and print them out, draw sketches, or even use silhouettes of your own photos. I've given instructions for a boy's cake — a break-dance design — and a ballet design for girls. Other themes could be tennis, skating, singing (imagine a glittery microphone and neon musical notes) or showjumping. This is a fabulous way to make a personalised cake for children, teens and — even big kids!

You will need:

20cm (8in) round Very Vanilla cake (see page 31), iced in powder blue/grey sugarpaste (for break-dance design) or white (for ballet design)

30cm (12in) round cake board, iced in a matching colour (see pages 23–25) or a cake stand

100g petal paste, in black (for break-dance) or pale flesh (for ballet)

Vodka or cooled boiled water

25g pale-pink petal paste (for ballet only)

Bright-lime, pink, yellow (primrose) and orange (tangerine) soft-peak royal icing (for break-dance) or dusky pink soft-peak royal icing (for ballet), in piping bags with No. 2 nozzles

White stiff-peak royal icing, in a piping bag with a small hole snipped in the end

Liquorice and claret paste colours (for ballet)

Piping gel (for ballet)

White non-toxic glitter (for ballet)

Ribbon, in your choice of colour

Equipment:

Plastic icing rolling pin

8 templates for break-dancers or ballerinas

Pastry brush

Small, sharp knife or palette knife

Small paintbrushes

Tutu template (for ballet design only)

Foam or gel pad

Cocktail sticks

STEP 1 Fix the cake centrally onto the cake board, if using, with a dab of royal icing to secure. To ensure your silhouettes are evenly spaced around the cake, wrap some ribbon around the cake, mark where it meets, then remove and measure it. Divide by eight and mark at equal intervals with a felt pen. Hold the ribbon back up to the cake and, above each pen-mark, make a tiny dot on the icing with a sharp knife, to indicate where to place the sugar silhouettes.

STEP 2 Roll out the black or flesh-coloured petal paste on a worktop dusted with icing suagr, to 1–2mm in thickness, or as thin as you can get without it becoming too fragile. Using the templates, cut out the eight different shapes and carefully brush the backs with some vodka or cooled boiled water. Just dampen, don't over-wet, or you may find that the liquid leaks out slightly.

TIP

If your shapes are a bit chunky and are slipping down the side of your cake once attached, use a cocktail stick to pierce through the centre of the shape and secure it onto the cake. You can remove the stick and fill in the hole with matching royal icing once it has dried out.

STEP 3 Lift each shape with a knife or palette knife and place them around the edges of the cake, spacing them equally.

STEP 4 Press the shapes lightly onto the icing with your fingertips to secure. If a shape slides down, you have probably made it too wet, so carefully peel away and dab off the excess with some kitchen paper. Once all the shapes are on your cake, leave to dry for a couple of hours.

STEP 5 Adding detail to your break-dancers is easy. Add flashes of colour with royal icing, as shown in the photo, to the shoes, hoodies and jackets. This is the final step if you are making a break-dancer cake, unless you wish to add a message to the top and ribbon round the base of the cake to finish.

STEP 6 For the ballerinas, paint shoes, bodices and tiny kissy lips onto the cut-outs with the paste colours and a small paintbrush. On a worktop dusted with icing sugar, roll out the pink petal paste thinly. Cut out eight tutu shapes using your template. On the foam pad, roll up the bottom half of each tutu with a cocktail stick, adding gentle pressure periodically to create a wavy frill at the bottom. This will help to give your design a 3D effect.

STEP 7 Pipe a strip of white royal icing onto the waist of each dancer. Attach the petal-paste skirts to the figures, securing on either side with a little more royal icing, and gently pressing to adhere them to the figures on the cake. Insert a cocktail stick on each side of the waist to hold the petal-paste tutus in place. Leave to dry overnight.

STEP 8 To finish, mix ½ teaspoon of piping gel with 1 teaspoon of white non-toxic glitter and paint this over the frilled tutus to make them sparkle. Finish by piping a message, if you wish, and adding ribbon to the base of the cake to hide the join with the board.

CAKE JAZZLING

One of my favourite latest inventions, this is a fabulous idea for teenagers. What's not to like about a glittery photo of yourself or one of your friends?! Here I have used a photo of my daughter; this is perfect for her 13th birthday. See page 163 for more details on printing photos onto edible paper. Use a clear photo that you can easily cut out — the face in this one covers about a 12–15cm (5–6in) area.

You can then use different-coloured glitters, lustres and piping gel to paint on sugary, glittery make-up detail. I also piped beads, pearls, hearts and shapes of royal icing onto plastic and scattered glitter over them whilst still wet. Once they had dried out, I lifted them from their plastic backing and used them to create beaded jewellery. I've made a hair accessory, necklace and earrings, but of course you can make anything; go for it and experiment. Hilarious, fun, and a little bit 'Essex', and the sparkliness will appeal to everyone!

You will need:

20cm (8in) round Very Vanilla cake (see page 31), iced in pink sugarpaste (see pages 71–8)

30cm (12in) round cake board, iced in red sugarpaste (see pages 71–78)

White stiff-peak royal icing (see page 52)

Different-coloured non-toxic glitters

1 large edible photo (use an edible-ink printer or see page 163)

Vodka or cooled boiled water

Metallic lustres (for the eyes and cheeks)

Piping gel

Blue soft-peak royal icing, in a piping bag with a No. 1.5 nozzle

Equipment:

Plastic document wallet

Piece of A4 card

Pastry brush

Greaseproof paper

Scissors

Small paintbrushes

Small, sharp knife

STEP 1 Begin by making your cake jazzles, so that these can dry overnight. They will set in a couple of hours but be careful handling them as they will still be soft inside. (For this cake I used several different-coloured glitters – EdAbleArt disco white, disco magenta, neon pink, purple, gold and green – to create the jazzly jewellery.)

STEP 2 Take the plastic document wallet and pop the piece of A4 card inside; this makes it easier to pick the wallet up when dusting off excess glitter.

STEP 3 Begin piping little pearls, beads and hearts (by piping two beads alongside each other and dragging downwards) of white royal icing onto the plastic wallet. I also piped some swirly 'S' shapes, to make the earrings in the photo. Very OTT!

STEP 4 Pipe one set of shapes at a time, in a line, then dust with your lightest colour of glitter, by loading up the pastry brush with glitter and tapping it over the piping on the wallet. You need to add lots of glitter to completely cover the piped shapes.

STEP 5 Dust off the excess by holding the wallet over a piece of greaseproof paper, tilting and gently tapping so that the excess glitter falls onto the paper. You can then use the paper as a funnel, folding up either side and tipping the glitter back into its pot.

STEP 6 Continue this with the next line of piped shapes and your next shade of glitter, pouring the excess back into the pots as you go. Once finished, leave the sparkly, glittering cake jazzles to set.

STEP 7 Attach the cake to the cake board and secure with a dab of royal icing. Carefully cut around the edge of the edible picture, and apply centrally to the top of the cake by brushing a little vodka or cooled boiled water onto the surface to stick the picture down.

STEP 8 Now you can start adding sugar 'make-up' to jazzle your photo. Using a small paintbrush, add some metallic lustre to the eyelids as eyeshadow, and as blusher to the cheeks.

STEP 9 Add some piping gel and glitter detail to the eyelids and lips to make them really glittery, so that they stand out. Finish the eyes with the blue royal icing to create luscious eyelashes.

STEP 10 Now attach your cake jazzles, lifting them off the wallet with a sharp knife and securing in place with a tiny dot of white royal icing under each bead, pearl or piped shape.

STEP 11 Finish off with a border of your choice.

PRINT-WRAP

Since I began my cake-decorating career, I think this must be one of my all-time favourite creations. Using gorgeous vintage edible print (from my friend Nikki at Francis-Dee), I am able to create an amazingly detailed look for this cake without having to hand-paint or pipe the fine detail. You can use any pattern to create a pretty design — there are plenty of free downloads online, or you can take a photo of fabric and print it off with an edible-ink printer, or send to a print company to turn it into a sheet of edible print. This cake is perfect for birthdays, weddings, tea parties or any time you fancy really!

You will need:

15cm (6in) round cake, iced in vintage-green sugarpaste (I used gooseberry paste colour) (see pages 71–8)

20cm (8in) round cake board, iced in the same colour (see page 23–5)

Approx. 100g white sugarpaste

Caramel–ivory–coloured stiff-peak royal icing (see page 52), in a piping bag with a No. 3 nozzle

2 x A4 sheets of edible print

Length of any ribbon, 2.5cm (1in) width, to use as a guide

Soft-jade satin ribbon, 1.5cm (1/2 in) width

Vodka or cooled boiled water

Gold lustre

Equipment:

Ribbon cutter (or ruler and scalpel)

Scissors

Small paintbrush

Pastry brush

STEP 1 Attach your cake centrally onto the board, with a dab of royal icing to secure.

STEP 2 Roll out your white sugarpaste to a long sausage, flatten and roll to a strip wide enough for your fabric wrap piece for the decorative band (This should be very thin – about 1-2mm). Cut your edible-print sheets lengthways in half and attach to the sugarpaste strip, which you have lightly brushed with some vodka or cooled boiled water. With a ribbon cutter set at the desired thickness or with a ruler and scalpel, cut your strip out; it should be approximately 2.5-3cm (1-1 1/2in) wide although if you prefer a thicker band that's fine as long as there is space for your ribbon and pearl trims.

STEP 3 Wrap the jade ribbon around the bottom of the cake and fasten it at the back with a tiny dot of icing. Then, following the top edge of

the jade ribbon, wrap the 2.5cm guide ribbon around the cake. The sugar print wrap can be aligned along its top edge so that it will be straight. A good tip is to roll it onto a small pin then unwrap over the sides of the cake (fasten it at the back with a tiny dot of royal icing).

STEP 4 Now use the paintbrush to paint vodka or cooled boiled water all around the cake, just above the guide ribbon so you have a sticky surface for your print wrap sugarpaste strip.

STEP 5 Attach the strip to the cake, with its best part at the front, laying it neatly onto the side of the cake, as straight as you can, just a fraction above the guide ribbon. Unwrapping from a pin is easiest; continue all the way round until you reach the starting point and cut with a sharp knife. Adhere by pressing onto your sticky cake or add a dab of stiff-peak royal icing to be sure it will stay.

STEP 6 Add pearl detail above and below the strip to finish, piping equal-sized beads of the caramel-ivory royal icing (see page 134). Leave to dry for at least two hours then add gold lustre to the pearls, mixed with vodka or cooled boiled water and painted onto the pearls to make them golden and gorgeous.

MODELLING

Hand-modelling is a really fun way to make cake decorations. Sugarpaste is a lovely medium for modelling, as it's very pliable and holds its shape well. If you wish, you can add a teaspoon of gum tragacanth to 500g sugarpaste and this will give you a better, firmer result, making your model set harder and firmer.

You can also model with chocolate paste and even with petal paste; they are both good mediums for rolling out, shaping and creating models. It's best to have a play around first; after a while you'll get the feel for it. Start simply, creating basic shapes that are made up of just a few parts.

FAIRYLAND MUSHROOM CAKE

Here I've made a whimsical, fairytale cake that is a perfect celebration cake for a little girl's party. The mushrooms conjure up some enchanting woodland magic!

You will need:

20cm (8in) round cake, iced in grass-green sugarpaste (I mixed gooseberry and leaf-green paste colours) (see pages 71–8)

30cm (12in) round cake board, iced in matching green sugarpaste

Approx. 700g white sugarpaste, with optional 2 tsp gum tragacanth, or sugar modelling paste

Red, caramel-ivory and spruce-green paste colours

Length of pink and green ribbon, 1.5cm width

White stiff-peak royal icing (see page 52), in a piping bag with a No. 3 nozzle

Green soft-peak royal icing, in a piping bag with a No. 2 nozzle

Pink royal icing, in a piping bag with a No. 2 nozzle

Selection of pre-made petal-paste blossom flowers (see page 145), in your choice of colours

Dust colours: green and white

Vodka or cooled boiled water

Selection of pre-made push-mould butterflies (see page 147)

White holographic non-toxic glitter

White soft-peak royal icing

Equipment:

Extra cake boards, for modelling and drying

Top smoother (optional)

Star nozzle

Cocktail stick (optional)

Small paintbrushes

Pastry brush

STEP 1 Colour approximately 300g of white sugarpaste with red paste colouring. Take around 100g for your large central mushroom and roll into a ball. Shape this into a cone by tapering one side by hand.

STEP 2 Invert, so that the wider base is on a cake board and push down with your hand to flatten the bottom. Pinch the top so that it looks more humpy and mushroom-like. Leave to set.

STEP 3 With the remainder of the red paste colour and repeat the previous steps to make a few more medium and small mushroom tops.

STEP 4 Make the mushroom stalks by kneading some caramel-ivory colouring into the remaining sugarpaste (about 200g)to get a putty-like colour. For the large mushroom, roll a fat sausage that's just over half the width of the base of the mushroom top. Do this by eye, as there's no need to be too precise. Turn the stalk over and press with the flat of your hand, or a top smoother, to flatten the top and bottom.

STEP 5 Make additional stalks in the same way to fit all the small mushroom tops. Leave them to dry on a cake board overnight.

STEP 6 Add the pink and green ribbon around the base of the cake (attach at the back with a dot of icing) and then add moss detail, by colouring approximately 200g sugarpaste with the dark-green colouring and hand-rolling it to make a few random moss clumps for around the cake edges. (Save some green sugarpaste for the top of the cake, too.) Press into these with the star nozzle to texturise and make them furrier and more moss-like.

STEP 7 Affix the large central mushroom stalk to the top of the cake with some stiff-peak royal icing. You may also want to use a cocktail stick in the base stalk to give extra support, but it's not essential. (If the cake is for a very young child, who will be eating it, it is better not to use a stick, but I would recommend using one if you are transporting the cake any distance.)

STEP 8 Add the top part of the large mushroom, fixing it with more royal icing, and add some moss detail to the base of the mushroom and a few bits around the top of the cake in the same way as you did to the sides. This will also help support the mushroom.

STEP 9 Add some piped tendrils of green royal icing dotted around the top and sides coming out from where you want your blossom flowers to be. Affix your petal-paste blossoms and place a few clumps of blossoms together on the top of your cake.

STEP 10 Affix the smaller mushroom stalks to the top of the cake board with royal icing, then add the mushroom tops. Leave to dry overnight or for at least a few hours.

STEP 11 Use a dry paintbrush to dust some of the green dust onto the moss to give it more depth. Mix the white dust with vodka or cooled boiled water to make a paste, and paint this onto the mushroom tops in white splodges.

STEP 12 Attach the butterflies to the large mushroom and the cake with some stiff-peak white royal icing and leave to set. Pipe blossom centres with the pink royal icing.

STEP 13 Use stiff-peak white and pink royal icing to pipe bodies onto the butterflies. Dust the entire cake with a small cascade of white holographic non-toxic glitter for a magical twinkly finish.

MULTI-TIER CAKES

BRUSH EMBROIDERY

If you find that piping with royal icing comes fairly easily (and enjoyably) to you, why not use freehand brush embroidery to create this elegant cake? For this classic design I have piped five-petal, three-petal and blossom freehand details to texturise the entire cake, then joined all the main floral parts together by piping stems, tendrils and leaves, and filled empty space with tiny triple pearls as pretty fillers. The tiers are finished with a satin ribbon.

As always, you can use any base colour to tailor the cake to your theme. If you find freehand piping tricky, mark out floral shapes randomly over the freshly iced cake tiers. Use cutters as guides for your main shapes. This design would also look stunning as a two-tier cake.

You will need:
15cm (6in), 23cm (9in) and 30cm (12in) round cakes, iced in powder-blue sugarpaste (see page 79)
2 x 38cm (15in) round cake boards, stuck together with Pritt stick, iced in matching powder-blue sugarpaste (see page 23–25)
The cakes should be stacked centrally on the iced boards so the cake is set before working on your piped design.

Ivory soft-peak royal icing (see page 52; use a tiny amount of caramel-ivory paste colour), in a piping bag with a No. 2 nozzle
Cooled boiled water
Ivory stiff-peak royal icing, in a piping bag with a No. 3 nozzle
Piping gel
Pearl lustre

Equipment:
Small paintbrushes
Kitchen paper
Ivory satin ribbon to finish each tier and edge your base boards, width 1.5cm (1/2 in)

STEP 1 Afix your ribbon around the tiers before commencing. Begin on the top of the upper tier and use the soft-peak ivory icing to pipe large five-petal floral patterns, randomly spaced. After piping each flower, immediately use a paintbrush dipped in cooled boiled water to embroider the edges (see page 136). If you leave the royal icing even for a couple of minutes it will start to skin over, so every time you pipe a flower, immediately brush in the edges then replace the brush in the water. Don't let your brush get too wet; if necessary, dry with kitchen paper.

STEP 2 After you have piped and embroidered your main large blooms, begin joining these up by piping stems, tendrils and leaf shapes. Add some thicker, pressure-piped tendrils in places, coming off the stems, and brush these down to embroider them onto the cake. You can embroider the larger tendrils in places, but leave the stems and leaves as unembroidered piped lines. Pipe centres in the floral shapes onto the connecting stems.

STEP 3 You can also pipe, and embroider, smaller floral shapes onto the connecting stems.

STEP 4 Once the top is nicely filled, continue down the sides of the top tier. Keep checking the space, and think about spacing out the flowers randomly and considering how they will flow and cascade over the tiers below. Make sure that some of the stems join up to the tier below so that the pattern becomes one and appears to flow even under the ribbon. Continue until all the tiers are covered with a medium to heavy lace coverage and the entire iced surface is texturised.

STEP 5 Now go back over the entire cake, checking for spaces into which you can pipe sets of triple dots. If you get snagging tails on these, gently press with the damp brush to neaten and round off the pearls.

BUTTERCREAM

This three-tier design is a simply beautiful and delicious celebration cake for a birthday or wedding. Finish the buttery icing with sugar hydrangeas, or use fresh flowers if you prefer (always take advice from your florist as to which flowers are safe to add to a cake, as some flowers can be toxic). A pretty alternative is to decorate a buttercream cake with vintage-style sugar roses or daisies.

I've used a three-tier stand with 20cm (8in), 25cm (10in) and 30cm (12in) plates, to accommodate my cakes and give me room to decorate the edges. You can of course make just one tier and place on a cake stand or an iced cake board at least 5cm (2in) larger than your cake.

You will need:
15cm (6in), 20cm (8in) and 25cm (10in) round cakes, iced in peach-coloured vanilla buttercream (see page 49)

Extra peach-coloured buttercream, in a piping bag with a No. 3 nozzle
Approx. 30 large, 30 medium and 50 small white petal-paste hydrangea flowers (see page 145)
Gooseberry-coloured soft-peak royal icing (see page 52), in a piping bag with a No. 2 nozzle
Green dust colour

Equipment:
Plastic piping bag for the buttercream snail trail
Small paintbrush

STEP 1 If you wish to texturise your buttercream for a special vintage look, you could scrape a tooth-edged side scraper all around each tier in one smooth dragging motion, while the buttercream is still soft, to create horizontal lines. Allow to set for a few hours. It looks good, but here I went with a flat buttercream covering.

STEP 2 If you are using a stand like mine, attach your cakes to each plate with a dab of stiff-peak royal icing. If making a single-tier cake, attach either to your cake stand or iced board (see introduction).

STEP 3 With your no. 3 nozzle bag, pipe a large snail trail of buttercream along the bottom edges of the cakes where they meet the stand or board, to neaten and add a pretty finishing touch.

STEP 4 Attach the petal-paste hydrangeas by piping a touch of buttercream to the underside of each one. Place them randomly over the tier(s), grouped together in some places to form heavier clumps. Leave to set for a couple of hours.

STEP 5 Dust the centres of the hydrangeas with a little green dust to add a realistic touch and then finish the centres by piping little collections of pearls in the middle of the flowers with the gooseberry-coloured royal icing.

COOKIE EXPLOSION

This is one of the most popular designs that we make at Fancy Nancy. You can create it in any colour and change the shapes of the cookies to tailor it for a man; red, white and blue is a great colour combination for men. This cake is sure to wow guests at any party. We even make these as wedding cakes sometimes!

You will need:

15cm (6in) round cake, iced in pink sugarpaste (I mixed pink and claret paste colour)

23cm (9in) round cake, iced in orange sugarpaste (I used tangerine paste colour)

35cm (14in) round cake board, iced in purple sugarpaste (I used Squires Kitchen purple, but you can mix blue and red, or use grape violet) (see page 23–5)

8 medium heart-shaped vanilla cookies (see page 44), decorated in orange, pink and purple with glitter and sprinkles, as shown

5 small heart-shaped vanilla cookies on sticks, decorated with sprinkles and glitter

Orange and pink stiff-peak royal icing, in piping bags with No. 3 nozzles

2 large heart-shaped vanilla cookies, iced with recipient's name and/or age, edge details piped in matching colours

Selection of smaller pre-decorated hearts to scatter over the cake

Selection of petal-paste blossoms, roses and daisies (see page 143), in your choice of colours

Stiff-peak royal icing, in a variety of colours, in piping bags with No. 2 nozzles

Equipment:

Scissors or wire cutters

Cocktail sticks (optional)

STEP 1 Begin by plunging your cookies (the ones with sprinkles), on their sticks, into the top tier. Set three slightly higher and further back and set two in front, as shown in the photo. You may need to cut the sticks down with strong scissors or wire cutters.

STEP 2 Fix the two piped cookies to decorate the front of your cake, attaching them with stiff-peak royal icing on the back of each cookie. If you find that the cookies slip off, use cocktail sticks under them to hold them in place until the icing sets.

STEP 3 Stick a selection of petal-paste flowers all around the top, edges and sides of the cakes, and onto the board, so that they cascade all over the place. Leave to set for a few hours or overnight.

STEP 4 Attach as many of your other pre-decorated hearts as you wish. The more the merrier!

STEP 5 Finish by piping royal-icing centres into your petal-paste flowers in a variety of colours.

WHEN A GIRL NEEDS CAKE

This cake is ideal for a girly shopaholic. It uses run-out decorations, which are easy to make (see page 129) and can be prepared in advance. If you want a different theme for any other birthday or personal celebration, choose two or three 'icons' that are special to the person. You could make 'bon voyage' cakes with icons from the country they are visiting or leaving; cakes for men with vintage robots, old-fashioned toys or sports, or fun run-out animal cakes for kids. Because you have done all the work making the run-outs in advance

You will need:

15cm (6in), 20cm (8in) and 25cm (10in) square cakes, iced in ivory sugarpaste, pre-stacked a day in advance (see pages 82–5 and 112–5)
35cm (14in) square cake board, iced in ivory sugarpaste (see pages 23–5), if required (I used a cake stand)

4 lengths of black grosgrain ribbon, width 1cm
3 iced run-outs (see page 129): margarita cocktail, high-heeled shoe and handbag shapes
White stiff-peak royal icing

STEP 1 Wrap a length of ribbon around each tier to hide the joins. Also attach a length of the ribbon to the edge of the cake board.

STEP 2 Attach the run-outs to the cake using some of the white royal icing to adhere them to the sugar paste icing. Place the shoe on the bottom-left of the base tier and the handbag just right of the centre on the middle tier. Finish with the cocktail placed left of the centre on the top tier. Simple, gorgous and chic!

VINTAGE BUTTON CAKE

This is one of my favourite cake designs. I came up with the idea a few years ago, inspired by my cousin Abby's gorgeous Jenny Packham wedding dress, which was embellished with beautiful mother-of-pearl buttons. I just knew that a cake decorated with these hand-made buttons would look lovely; indeed, it is a really popular choice for weddings and other celebrations. I love the antique-pink colour scheme, but the base works equally well in ivory for a more traditional look, or you can choose any soft pastel colour to suit your theme. Making the sugar buttons is very simple and can be done well in advance. The finishing touches are the pearl lustre — it makes them look so realistic — and the final iced stitch, which gives the effect that the buttons are sewn directly onto the surface of the cake. Stunning! Because the cake is so heavily embellished with sugar decorations, if you have the odd undulation or bump, you can cleverly disguise any imperfections with a button and it will still look perfect.

SERVES AROUND 150, IN SMALL CAKE-TASTING PORTIONS

You will need:

15cm (6in), 20cm (8in), 25cm (10in) and 30cm (12in) round cakes, iced in marzipan and antique-pink sugarpaste (I use a tiny amount of pink paste colour and gradually knead in a tiny addition of egg-yellow), stacked centrally on the board as a one-piece cake a day in advance of decorating (see pages 112–115)

2 x 40cm (16in) round cake boards, stuck together with Pritt stick, iced in matching antique-pink sugarpaste (see page 23–5)

Approx. 3 metres of ivory satin ribbon, 10mm width

Icing sugar

Approx. 500g petal paste

Pale pink soft-peak royal icing (see page 52), in two piping bags (no more than half-full), with No. 1.5 and No. 2 nozzles

Topaz lustre dust (I use Squires Kitchen 'Moon Beams')

Piping gel

Cooled boiled water

Equipment:

Plastic icing rolling pin

Floppy mat (or book wrapped in cling film)

3 circle plunger cutters: small, medium and large

2 extra piping nozzles, a No. 1.5 and a No. 2 (old ones are best, as cutting buttonholes wears them out)

Foam or gel pad

Ball tool

Extra cake board

Small, sharp knife

Pastry brushes

Small paintbrush (No. 4 artist's brush)

HOW TO MAKE THE MOTHER-OF-PEARL BUTTONS

STEP 1 You can make these buttons well in advance, as they last for months. This makes approximately 150 small, 100 medium and 100 large sugar buttons.

STEP 2 Dust the worktop with icing sugar and knead the petal paste until soft and pliable.

STEP 3 You will need to roll out just a small amount of petal paste at a time, as it dries out very quickly. You will also need to keep the rest of the rolled-out sheet covered whilst you are working on each batch of buttons. I recommend a floppy mat for this – a clear piece of tough plastic that you can lay over the petal paste – otherwise a book wrapped in cling film will do.

STEP 4 Take approximately 50g petal paste and roll out thinly until the worktop underneath starts to show through. Aim for no more than 1mm thickness. Petal paste is very stretchy and goes a long way, and you need to use quite a bit of pressure to roll it out, as it's much firmer and more elastic than regular sugarpaste.

STEP 5 Cut out the buttons with the round cutters; do just one size to begin with, and just a few at a time so that they don't dry out. (Once you get quicker at shaping them, you can cut out more at once – I do about 20 at a time.) Press the cutter down firmly into the paste to ensure you get a clean cut with no rough edges.

STEP 6 Once you have cut out a few circles, cover the rest of your sheet with the floppy mat, then use one of the extra piping nozzles (No.1.5 for the small buttons, or No.2 for medium and large) to push out two little holes in each button, equally spaced in the middle of the circle.

STEP 7 Now take one button and lay it on the foam pad. Using the ball modelling tool, carefully press around the inside of the outer edge with gentle, even pressure, moving it around one way then back the other until your circle has formed a little upturned edge and looks like a real button. Pick up the button with your fingers, gently holding the edge, and put it onto a cake board.

STEP 8 Continue in this way, cutting out just a few circles at once, and covering the remaining petal paste while you cut the holes and mould the edges. Do all the small ones first, then the medium and finally the large. Keep them in separate groups and line them up on the cake board so that they are easy to keep count of.

I use little plunger polka dot cutters from Kemper for quickness; they generally come in a set of five different sizes and I use the small, medium and large ones.

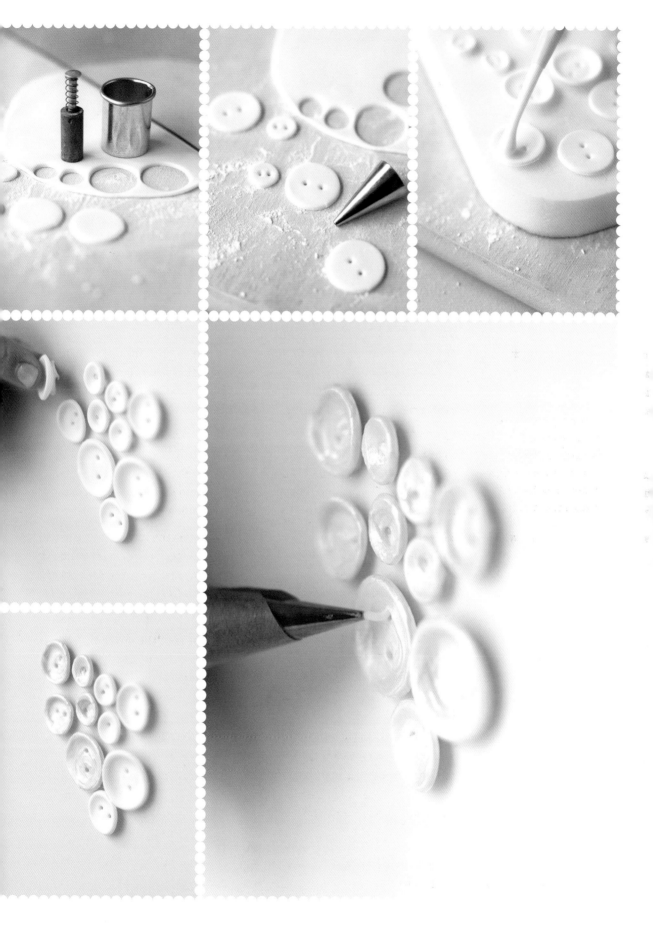

STEP 9 Leave to dry for at least 24 hours before using them to decorate the cake, but ideally you can make them several days or weeks in advance. When dry, tip them into a box or container (not airtight or they may go soft) and leave in a cool, dry place until you are ready to decorate the cake.

HOW TO ASSEMBLE THE REST OF THE CAKE

STEP 1 Have your pre-iced cakes ready and stacked the day before you want to begin decorating. Also make sure that your buttons are prepared as described above, at least 24 hours in advance. Adhere the ribbon to the cake before commencing sticking on buttons as it is good to slightly overhang some parts of the ribbon to avoid formal lines.

STEP 2 To apply the buttons to the cake, I like to work from the top tier downwards, to avoid knocking any buttons off the tiers below. It takes me a couple of hours to stick all the buttons onto a three-tier cake of this size, but if you are a beginner, give yourself a bit longer; don't rush your masterpiece!

Before lustering the buttons, I like to check that there are no odd bits of icing sugar or dust on the cake. Use a pastry brush to dust over the cake and buttons. You must do this before you pearlise them, as you can't use a pastry brush after pearlising because the gel is quite sticky and pastry-brush hairs will stick to the buttons.

STEP 3 'Glue' each button on, by piping a blob of soft-peak ivory royal icing (from the bag with the No. 2 nozzle) onto the back of it – taking care not to pipe over the holes – then gently pressing the button onto the cake's icing. You need only the lightest touch, as the royal icing will easily adhere the button. (They will set rock hard by the next day.) If at any stage you think you want to move a button that doesn't look right, just take a sharp knife and gently scrape down behind the button – it will come off easily.

STEP 4 Apply the buttons following the photographs as a guide. Heavily embellish the base tier with fewer buttons towards the top. This creates a lovely cascading effect.

STEP 5 Once you have attached all of your buttons, they can be left to dry on the cake for a couple of hours before continuing with the next step.

STEP 6 In a small bowl, gently mix together a teaspoon of the topaz lustre and two teaspoons of piping gel.

STEP 7 Now you can begin painting the buttons, using a small paintbrush to paint over the middle and just up onto the edges of each button. You don't have to paint right round the edge, and be careful not to paint any gel onto the icing, or the cake will look messy. Start from the top of the cake and work your way down. It takes me a couple of hours to paint them all; you might need longer if you're a beginner.

STEP 8 Next is my favourite stage, and it really makes the cake. To add the 'stitches', you need the piping bags of pink soft-peak royal icing – use the bag with a No. 2 nozzle for the medium and large buttons, and the No. 1.5 nozzle for the small buttons. Again, start from the top and work your way downwards. Stitch onto each medium and large button by squeezing a small line of royal icing from the top hole to the lower one. When you touch the lower hole with the nozzle, stop squeezing and pull away from the cake.

STEP 9 Once you have added stitches to all the medium and large buttons, go back over the cake, again from the top downwards, this time stitching the remaining small buttons with your No. 1.5 nozzle. You are finished, so sit back and marvel at your gorgeous cake!

If you stir the gel and lustre mixture too quickly, it goes everywhere, so don't do it near the cake! Stir it slowly and gently to avoid a cloud of shimmery topaz going all over your workspace.

When you get good at piping, you can avoid getting snags or tails (or nipples as they are known in the trade!). Until then, don't worry if a little bit of icing is sticking up on your 'stitches' – you can make it look neat by using a small pastry brush dipped in cooled boiled water. Gently press the damp brush onto the icing to push down the icing snugly into the buttonhole and create the 'stitched on' effect.

CAKETASTROPHES!

There are some things that can go wrong when cake decorating; I like to call these 'caketastrophes'! In this section I outline cake mishaps, things to avoid when decorating cakes or cookies, and how to solve problems where possible. When cakes go wrong, especially when you are a beginner, it feels terribly dramatic and scary, and there's a sense of panic that if you don't fix it quickly, it will be ruined. Or worse, you may want to throw it all away after hours of painstaking labour.

Keep a cool head and you can normally fix things and save your cakes. At the very least, you could change the design and add more detail to cover up any accidents; then no one will ever know! A good point to mention again here is that cake decorating does take time. Allow yourself enough time for your projects because this will help to avoid any caketastrophes caused by rushing.

I haven't found any cake decorating books that tell you what may go wrong, how to pre-empt particular problems, or more importantly, how you can fix them. So, throughout this book, I've referred to possible annoyances, and here I list some more tricky things to watch out for and ways to rectify these irritating caketastrophes.

So keep calm: you can probably fix it, and if you can't fix it, you can probably disguise it or, at worst, you can strip off your cake coverings and begin again – not ideal, but still saveable. You only learn by making mistakes.

HAIRLINE CRACKS

On occasion, once you have stacked your masterpiece and are starting to decorate, you will notice one or two (or even more!) hairline cracks. This is an indication either that you haven't put enough cake dowels into the cake, or that some may have gone in at a slight angle. After time, the upper cakes will push down on the base tier and may start to cause these cracks.

The best way to avoid this happening in the first place is to never skimp on dowels. The heavier the cakes are, and the more tiers they have, the more dowels you will need; e.g. for a small 15cm (6in) top tier, you will need at least 5–6 dowels in the cake below it. But in a 30cm (12in) base tier that has 25cm (10in) and 15cm (6in) cakes above it, you will need 12–14 dowels, and I recommend that they are the heavy-duty type. It's easy to forget to put them in, or to just put too few, but they are really important.

Once hairline cracks have appeared, there are a couple of ways you can solve or improve them. If your cake is finished, it will probably be okay, as you'll have been working on it for a couple of days and it will have already survived any transportation, so simply fill over the cracks with royal icing. When done well, this will almost vanish away the evidence. Another solution is to take some of the sugarpaste with which you covered your cake (a particularly good idea if you've blended a special colour, as it will be difficult to match perfectly with royal icing) and work this into a paste with some cooled boiled water until it has the consistency of soft-peak royal icing. With a clean finger, smooth the paste over and into any cracks. Then carefully remove any excess with a small, sharp knife and good-quality kitchen paper (one that doesn't shed any bits) or use a brand-new cloth to do this. Allow to dry and your cracks will be well hidden or, if you've done a good job, almost completely gone!

However, if large cracks start appearing soon after stacking, this is a sign that your top tiers are too heavy and you haven't doweled the cake correctly. You can either carefully lift the tiers off, using a knife to cut them apart so that the icing on the tier below isn't pulled away from the cake, then add lots more dowels. Bear in mind that it's easy to damage the icing at this stage. Or sometimes it's a good idea to wait and check the progress, as the cracks may not get any worse, in which case you can simply fill them with icing as described above, or if there is a large amount of decoration going onto the cake, for example a rose corsage, you can strategically place models or run-outs over the cracks.

ROGUE AIR BUBBLES

If you find a very annoying air bubble occurring under sugarpaste a couple of days after beginning decoration (this can particularly occur when there are big changes in temperature) the only thing you can do is to scrape off the decoration, insert a pin tool into the bubble in a few places and carefully press down the iced cake covering to flatten. This will probably cause a few cracks. Make up some royal icing, matching the colour as closely as possible to your sugarpaste. Or if you have any leftover sugarpaste from the covering, use water to wet some down into a paste with the consistency of soft-peak royal icing. Using a clean fingertip, smooth this over the cracks and carefully wipe away any excess with a piece of just-damp kitchen paper, then dry with a clean piece. Leave to set for a few hours and then redecorate. Once the cake is decorated this should not show too much, but if you decide you want to reposition your cake so that this area is at the back, re-attach ribbon (if you are using one) so that the join occurs beneath it, making this the back of the cake. .

CAKE SWEATING

Humidity in the air or changes of temperature (for example, if your sponge has been chilled in a fridge then quickly iced), can cause a 'sweaty' look on the icing, called cake sweating. Don't be tempted to dry this or even to touch it or you'll create smears, marks or, worse, damage to the decoration.

Move the cake to a room where the temperature is regular and constant. After a few hours, the surface should dry out again. I've had this happen a few times during summer months and had to move cakes into an air-conditioned room, as sugarpaste doesn't react well to being chilled. Another good idea is to use a dehumidifier in the room in which you are working on and storing your cake.

LEAKAGE

On occasion, if you have a really syrupy cake and it's a hot time of year, you may notice some juicy, sugary leaks coming out from the bottom of the cake tiers, either onto the tier below or onto the cake board. If your cake has ribbon around it, you may find that the leak has marked the ribbon. You will need to replace it with a fresh length, but for now remove the ribbon entirely while you fix the problem. If you have piped an iced pearl trail or bead trim, you'll have to carefully cut away the part where the sugary syrup is leaking out.

To rectify this problem, use good-quality kitchen paper to soak up the leaking syrup as soon as possible. Otherwise it will start to eat into the icing on the cake below or the iced board. Take a piece of kitchen paper and very gently press onto the area to soak up some of the moisture. Lift the paper away, taking care not to smudge it onto the cake as you do this. Repeat with fresh pieces of paper until all the moisture has gone. Keep checking regularly over a period of time, as it may leak a bit more. If it's a light-coloured cake, you can also dust over a little icing sugar to dry out the area.

Once you are certain the leaking has stopped, you can re-attach the ribbon or pipe back into the space in the pearl trim or snail trail. If the damage is bad, the best option might be to cover the area with additional sugar decorations, for example flowers or butterflies, etc.

COLOUR BLEEDING

This is when one colour of icing runs or spreads into another; lighter-coloured icings can get stained by stronger ones. This happens most commonly with combinations of light and dark, especially on royal icing run-outs or when you pipe onto a freshly iced surface. To avoid this caketastrophe, make sure that you allow a colour or icing to dry for 24 hours before continuing to decorate or fill with a darker colour.

COLOUR BLOTCHES

Sometimes, if you haven't mixed your paste colours thoroughly, particularly for run-outs and cookie decorating, strong blotches of colour can appear. There's nothing you can do about this once the icing has dried, but if you notice it happening, split your icing bag and carefully remix. This is due to under-mixing; make sure you can't see any spots of colour and you have a smooth, all-over colour in your sugarpaste or royal icing.

CRUMBLY ICING ON COOKIES

This is where you have over-mixed your royal icing, which leads to a crumbly, spongy texture. The cookie decoration will crumble off, especially if you put the cookies in cookie bags. If this happens, you may want to leave it but take care not to knock the decoration. Alternatively, you can cut off the decoration with a sharp knife, bake the cookies again on a low temperature – around 140°C/ Gas mark 1 – for a few minutes to crisp them back up, then you can just ice over the surface again once cool. This is better than throwing the whole lot away.

PIPING OVER SNAGS, HOLES AND GAPS

Royal icing is a fabulous 'edible Polyfiller'! If you have had to prick air bubbles, pick off bits of decoration or have found a gap anywhere on your cake, you may be left with a hole to cover. Most designs allow for you to disguise these with your decoration, but if not (e.g. when you're piping stripes, if you want a clean iced surface, or if when you come to add your ribbon there's a bumpy hole), you can just pipe over these with stiff-peak royal icing to fill the void, gap or hole. Scrape away the excess and you're left with a smooth surface on which to begin your decorating.

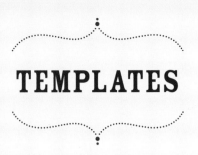

TEMPLATES

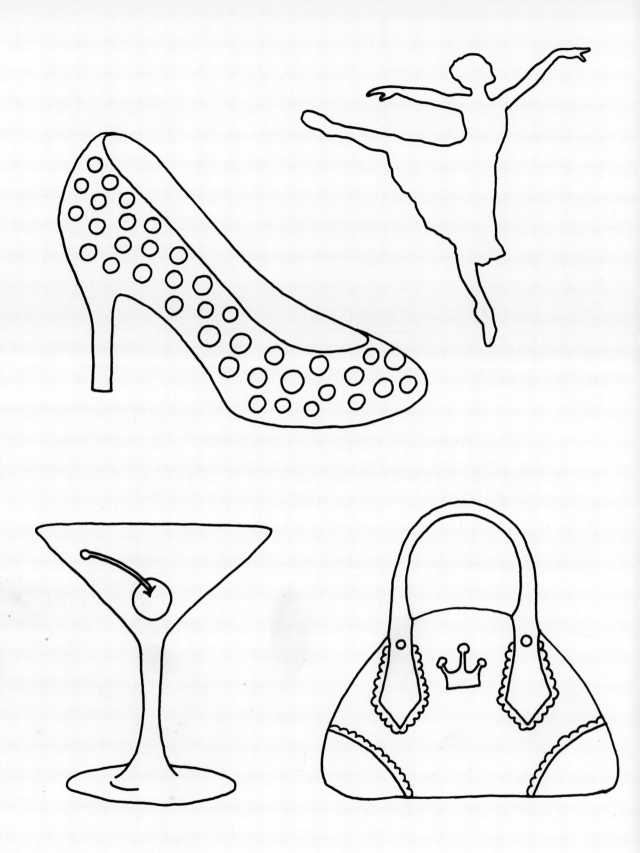

STOCKISTS

For general cake decorating edibles, supplies and equipment:

ALMOND ART
Units 15/16 Faraday Close
Gorse Lane Industrial Estate
Clacton-on-Sea
Essex CO15 4TR
www.almondart.com
Tel: 01255 223 322

CAKES, COOKIES AND CRAFTS
Unit 2
Francis Business Park
White Lund Industrial Estate
Morecambe
Lancashire LA3 3PT
www.cakescookiesand
craftsshop.co.uk
Tel: 01524 389 684

PICTURE THIS
8 Matlock Way
Canvey Island
Essex SS8 0EW
Tel: 01268 684 547

SPLAT COOKING
Splat Cooking Stuff Limited
PO Box 83
Princes Risborough
Buckinghamshire
HP27 9WB
www.splatcooking.net
Tel: 0870 766 8290

SQUIRES KITCHEN
Squires Group Squires House
3 Waverley Lane
Farnham
Surrey GU9 8BB
www.squires-shop.com
Tel: 0845 617 1810 or
 01252 260 260

SUGARSHACK
Unit 12
Bowmans Trading Estate
Westoreland Road
London NW9 9RL
www.sugarshack.co.uk
Tel: 020 8204 2994

For baking ingredients, chocolate and packaging:

KEYLINK
Keylink Limited
Green Lane
Ecclesfield
Sheffield S35 9WY
www.keylink.org
Tel: 0114 245 5400

For gorgeous stationery, party and wedding accessories and print design:

FRANCIS-DEE
140 Woodside
Leigh-On-Sea
Essex SS9 4RE
www.francis-dee.co.uk
Tel: 01702 520961

Also, a huge thanks to all the fantastic companies who kindly let us use their products in the photographs:

BOMBAY DUCK
231 The Vale
London W3 7QS
Tel: 020 8749 3000
www.bombayduck.co.uk

THE CROCKERY CUPBOARD
www.thecrockerycupboard.co.uk
Tel: 07966 235 521 or
07974 636 127

DOTCOMGIFTSHOP
Unit 3-4 Allied Way
London W3 0RL
www.dotcomgiftshop.com
0208 746 2473

ETSY
www.etsy.com

JOHN LEWIS
www.johnlewis.com
Tel: 08456 049 049

NOT ON THE HIGH STREET
www.notonthehighstreet.com

PEACH BLOSSSOM
www.peachblossom.co.uk

ROSES ALL OVER
www.rosesallover.co.uk

INDEX

THANKS

This book is a dream come true, but it didn't just happen by magic. I have so many people to thank for their help in turning it into a reality. I would not have been able to develop a successful cake business, let alone write a book, without the support of Simon 'my rock, my soul mate and all that cheesy stuff from our fave Steve Wright Sunday show!' and his help throughout my cakey career. Simon, sorry that you had to endure days and days of trawling through my text before I sent it in to Ebury, but now you are a cake expert and I am sure find the subject completely thrilling! Thanks to our gorgeous children, Ruby, Lydia and George for putting up with my stressyitis, being ever humorous and so understanding.

Then the rest of my family: I want to thank my dad, George, who is a total legend and helps us all in so many ways both at home and at the shop, everyday, doing deliveries, washing up, checking the cakes are level (listening to Django Reinhardt and drinking all the cake brandy). Thanks to Mum, too, for everything! My 'mother-in-law' Lydia, is one of my best friends and an inspiration. I can't thank her enough for all that she does for us, from childcare, life coaching to the business accounts – and even clearing out my messy handbag! Thanks to Nancy for being a FABULOUS sister and super auntie to our kids, especially Ruby, who is your mini-me.

Thanks to the brilliant Christine Lee, my cake mentor and true friend, for teaching me so much about the wonderful world of cake decorating and making it all hilarious fun – we are a great double act! Big thanks to Dena Robles who worked with me in the early days to produce amazing cake photos and more; a great friend and a talented photographer whom we miss very much now that you have headed back to the USA with your gorgeous family.

The support of my extended family has also been crucial: Auntie Carol who made cakes for me when I was little, naughty Brenda, Uncle Fred and all the aunties, uncles and cousins who I don't see enough of. Also thanks for the assistance from so many kind friends, particularly Lucy Norris, my oldest and closest friend, for her loyalty and calming influence; Ali Harris for her support and introduction to *Wedding* magazine and for helping with this book; the talented and creative Louise Naomi Best for my Fancy Nancy logo and more; Dan Carter for coming into Fancy Nancy and making some seriously awesome cakes; Kate and Craig for their wonderful photography; Michelle and Pete for my website; and friends-and-ex-colleagues Rosie Shorten and Colin Chih. Thanks to Mich Turner for giving me a job at Little Venice Cake Company back in the day – an opportunity for which I am ever grateful.

BIG thanks and hugs to my agents, Jennifer Christie and Jane Graham Maw, who believed in me, and my baking passions, and supported me throughout the making of this book. And to all my staff at Fancy Nancy: Olivia Kerr, Tara Carter, Georgia Coles, Sam Sains and Ali Penn-Franzolin. Enormous thanks, also, to the team at Smith and Gilmour: Alex, Emma, Gavin and Rose – and to Maja Smend for her gorgeous shots, and to the stylist (and stylish!) Ali Lovett; I have had the best time working with you on this book. And a big thank you to Paul Tait.

Thanks to magazine editors Victoria Sullivan and Catherine Westwood for supporting me since the early days. Thanks to Nikki Stock for allowing me to use her beautiful prints on my cakes and in this book, and to my wonderfully exuberant TV agents Kim Farmer and Kirsty Williams of Insanity Management. And grateful thanks to the enthusiastic team at Ebury: to Kasi Collins, Katie Hall, Laura Herring and Imogen Fortes.

And, of course, thanks to all my customers, twitter, blog and facebook followers and the readers of my book for all your support. I would be lost without you.